The Secrets of

Gluten-Free
BAKING

The Secrets of

Gluten-Free BAKING

DELICIOUS

—∞—

WHOLE FOOD

—∞—

RECIPES

JILLAYNE CLEMENTS

FRONT TABLE BOOKS • AN IMPRINT OF CEDAR FORT, INC. • SPRINGVILLE, UTAH

DISCLAIMER

The information in this book is not intended to diagnose, treat, or cure illness or disease and is not intended to be used as a replacement for proper medical attention. Consult your health care professional before changing your diet.

Text and images © 2013 by Jillayne Clements
All rights reserved.

No part of this book may be reproduced in any form whatsoever, whether by graphic, visual, electronic, film, microfilm, tape recording, or any other means, without prior written permission of the publisher, except in the case of brief passages embodied in critical reviews and articles.

ISBN: 978-1-4621-1286-9

Published by Front Table Books, an imprint of Cedar Fort, Inc., 2373 W. 700 S., Springville, UT 84663
Distributed by Cedar Fort, Inc., www.cedarfort.com

Library of Congress Cataloging-in-Publication Data on file.

Cover and page design by Erica Dixon
Cover design © 2013 by Lyle Mortimer
Edited by Shelby Law

Printed in the United States of America

10 9 8 7 6 5 4 3 2 1

To Grandma,

Who will always be remembered for your delicious home-cooked meals and for making each person in your circle of friends and family feel special.

You are deeply missed.

PRAISE FOR THE SECRETS OF
Gluten-Free
BAKING

"I am so impressed with this beautiful book! Jillayne has taken all the guesswork out of understanding the "How to's" of gluten-free cooking. Wow! Can it be easier to understand? She has done all your homework for you in finding a way to get through all the modern, man-made stuff we call "food" and teaches us with her wit and wisdom little treasures of knowledge on understanding how it all works—and how to do it yourself. I've known Jillayne for many years and seen the marvelous results of her many efforts in making wholesome and nutritious foods, let alone this magnificent insight to help us all understand the intricacies concerning gluten intolerance and what we "CAN DO" about it. This is must for anyone needing a "How to—Gluten-Free and Still Tastes Good" book.

Renae J. Spencer
Young Living Family Farm

"I have seen thousands of patients suffering from Celiac Disease, Hashimoto's Disease, and other autoimmune conditions who are unable to use gluten-free baking recipes because they lack the fiber content needed to help with proper digestion and because they typically have a higher level of refined starches, gums, fats, and sugars. This in turn causes many other metabolic imbalances throughout the patient's body and digestive tract. Jillayne Clements does an amazing job using a combination of whole food ingredients—which makes gluten-free baking easier, tastier, but most importantly, healthier. I definitely recommend this book."

Joshua Redd, DC, DABFM
Chiropractic Physician, Certified & Diplomate in Functional Medicine
Lowthyroid101.com

Contents

Acknowledgments

Thank you, Mom, Dad, Jen, and Jax, for your help with this cookbook, for your support and encouragement, and for being there for me through all the craziness. Conner and Adria, thanks for your help, and to you and the rest of the family, thanks for recipe feedback and support.

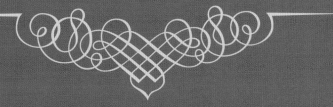

ALSO AVAILABLE

The DIET Rebel's Cookbook

Eating CLEAN and GREEN

JILLAYNE CLEMENTS and
MICHELLE STEWART

Section One

Introduction
The Day My Gluten-Free Life Began

"You will never be able to eat anything with gluten for the rest of your natural life. EVER."

That's what my doctor told me while I was sitting in his office with my jaw on the ground. I didn't know whether to cry out of frustration or sigh in relief, because his diagnosis could be the missing link to why I still had so many Hashimoto's thyroiditis symptoms—symptoms that persisted even with medication and a good diet.

"What about sprouted wheat?" I asked. "It partially digests gluten, so I can tolerate it better."

"Not even that," he said. "Not even crumbs of anything with wheat, rye, or barley."

No wheat, rye, or barley for the rest of my life? No sourdough pancakes or pizza crust, no sprouted wheat bread fresh out of the oven? In my mind, this meant no more enjoyment of food.

Still in a mind fog, whether from the news of needing to eat gluten-free (or GF) for the rest of my life or because mind fog is just a part of Hashimoto's, I quit eating gluten-containing foods cold turkey. The only problem was that I absolutely refused to eat the premade gluten-free products and mixes made with white rice flour, potato and tapioca starch, and xanthan gum that make up the bulk of the gluten-free diet (which costs $7.00 for a small package of mix or loaf of dry, hard-to-swallow bread, but that's just a side note). The reasons I refused to eat such pre-packaged food were as follows: 1) All the starch would cause me to be hyper one minute and crying the next; 2) I was unsure of the nutrient and fiber content in those packages, but I was willing to bet fifty-three Lavender Berry Cream Pies that they weren't as nutritious as sprouted wheat; 3) I wondered how much phytic acid (protection on all sleeping state nuts, grains, seeds, and beans that bind with nutrients like calcium, magnesium, copper, iron, and zinc, and carries them right out of your body)[1] was in just one of those little packages because they hadn't been soured or germinated; and 4) I wouldn't resort to eating refined food out of a box after writing, creating recipes for, and living by the principles in a cookbook dedicated to whole, natural, and properly prepared food—*The Diet Rebel's Cookbook: Eating Clean and Green*, coauthored with Michelle Stewart. So my options were starving, becoming a grain-free faddist, or creating my own gluten-free food using whole food ingredients. The stubborn, optimistic side of me thought, "I'll make my own gluten-free, whole food recipes, and then I'll put them in another cookbook. After all, there is a virtual hole in the market for whole and gluten-free food, even more so for properly prepared (soaked or soured) whole and gluten-free food, and I bet I can make these whole food recipes for less money than the premade goods at the stores."

Therefore, I began my pioneering adventure of making whole and gluten-free foods with ingredients that seemed more familiar. I would

Often what I would dream in my mind—a beautiful creation that was both nourishing and delicious—turned out less than appetizing because I was experimenting with "alternative flours" with unknown results.

love to say that everything went perfectly in this experimentation, but it didn't. That's because often what I would dream in my mind—a beautiful creation that was both nourishing and delicious—turned out less than appetizing because I was experimenting with "alternative flours" with unknown results. For instance, buckwheat, a gluten-free seed, though relatively healthy, tastes more like blechwheat, and amaranth tastes like dirt, which doesn't bode well for a household of hungry people.

Once, with a marvelous recipe in my mind using bean flour, I set out to make muffins.

Now, taste is very important for me, so naturally I'm the kind of gal that likes to taste things as I make them. But being a novice in the gluten-free world, I didn't know how horrible uncooked bean flour was until I about gagged while tasting a bit of batter. I just hoped the taste would bake out.

Using lots of baking soda in the muffin batter—so the muffins would rise—I placed my muffins in the oven to cook. A half hour later, I smelled burning and realized that muffin batter had poured over the edges of the tins and covered the bottom of my oven. Strangely enough, the muffins—though they were a lot smaller because half of the batter was still in the bottom of the oven—tasted decent. Apparently, bean flour does lose some of the overpowering flavor during cooking. Not all of it, though.

Fast-forward three days. I was preparing dinner for guests, and I wanted everything to turn out just right, which included eating at the dining room table with nice dishes instead of eating at the snack bar with chipped dishes and utensils that may have taken a spin in the garbage disposal. Dinner was promising—portabello mushrooms and cheese over meat along with Texas cheese fries. Half an hour into cooking time, my kids informed me that there was a fire in the oven. Apparently, I forgot to clean up the spilled muffin batter from a few days before, and it was flammable. Luckily, it burned itself out, and our guests didn't even suspect that the smoke flavor that only added to the fries wasn't there on purpose.

So one batch of GF muffins turned into a disaster, but that didn't mean that everything from that point would. My next project was sourdough bread made with certified gluten-free rolled oats that I ground into flour. I mixed the flour with water and a little raw apple cider vinegar and let it sit on my counter, only to realize a day later that precooked grain—rolled oats are steamed—doesn't sour like other uncooked grains. Instead, it grows mold as well as, if not better than, a petri dish.

With time, my gluten-free cooking improved, especially when I discovered a couple of things that saved my cooking life. I began using certified gluten-free oats and flax to use as a binder/stabilizer, cooked beans that I sprouted before cooking for added nutrition and ease of digestion, and the biggest miracle of them all, the gluey texture of sprouted and cooked brown rice and sweet rice that I then dehydrated and ran through my grain mill to turn into flour. I never had the need to use xanthan gum or potato or tapioca starch.

With these new ingredients in mind, I made my first batch of whole grain rolls. They tasted

> With time, my gluten-free cooking improved, especially when I discovered a couple of things that saved my cooking life.

divine because they tasted like sprouted wheat rolls fresh from the oven. I hadn't had them in such a long time, I didn't even care that they fell to pieces on my plate. In subsequent batches, though, I fixed that little problem while keeping the flavor intact.

Muffins and cupcakes turned out wonderfully well with cooked beans as a base. My kids even said they tasted as good as the "bad" kind, which means they tasted as good as the processed kind they know aren't good for them. This was a huge improvement over the time they begged me to make something from sprouted wheat, saying, "Please, we'll even grind our own wheat."

With additional discoveries and more successful experiments, I had a sufficient number of recipes, including pie crusts, pizza crusts, rolls, cream puffs, muffins, and more to keep my family fed. In my mind, this was a small miracle because I was again able to feed my family food that nourished their bodies while at the same time tasting wonderful.

One outstanding bonus to all this whole food, gluten-free cooking is that I got my brain back! Whether or not eating gluten-free was the basis for this or if it was taking a steady dosage of thyroid supplement along with hefty amounts of iron supplementation, I may never know.

What I do know is that my kids complement me again on my cooking. Do they still miss the things I used to make with sprouted wheat? They actually don't anymore, especially after I learned how to make crackers. However, there's a small part of me that hopes my body will heal of this whole gluten issue and I can enjoy gluten-containing things again. Until then, GF in our house stands for Great Food, and my wish is for you to experience the same.

Jillayne Clements

What This Cookbook Is

This cookbook was born from the idea of wanting GF substitutes for gluten containing baked goods like bread, pizza crust, cookies, or crackers. Along the way, I discovered some pretty awesome secrets about gluten-free baking that I wanted to share with others. That is, I have learned to cook gluten-free without the use of the traditional gluten-free baking essentials (that is, tapioca flour, potato starch, and xanthan gum), instead using only whole food, "normal" ingredients. This has resulted in gluten-free baked goods that look and taste and feel more like wheat than traditional gluten-free items.

Whether you're on a temporary or permanent gluten-free diet, you'll find this cookbook helpful if you wish to nourish your body through whole and mostly properly prepared whole grains including brown rice, certified gluten-free oats, teff, cooked beans, and flax. Please make sure your doctor gives you the okay to eat certified gluten-free oats and/or flax before trying any of the recipes using them. Some people may not tolerate them well.

What This Cookbook Is Not

A book filled with your typical white rice, potato starch, and high-glycemic trying-to-pass-off-cardboard-as-actual-food cookbook. Chances are, if you have celiac disease or major gluten issues, you already know what it is and the symptoms that go along with it, so they will not be discussed in this book. However, there are many good sources on the topic that you may find helpful. Chances are, also, that you already know all about gluten and its amazing ability to bind and trap gasses for rising bread, and that it's hidden in all sorts of foods like salad dressings, canned soups, chili, and so on, which is another perk to making your own food.

Section Two

Secrets of Making Gluten-Free Products That Taste like Wheat

When it comes to baking gluten-free, for the most part, it just isn't the same as good, old-fashioned wheat products that we're so used to eating. This is partly due to taste, partly to the texture, and partly to the satiety that comes when you've just eaten a slice of home-made, whole-grain bread, along with the nutrients and fiber that come with it. When substituting all this goodness with refined starches, you may get a similar texture to refined white bread, but satiety, fiber, and nutrients are certainly lacking. Other times, there's a lot of grit or just unfamiliar flavors that take getting used to.

There's a solution to these issues, and that's what I'll be sharing with you throughout the pages of this book.

Secret #1 | Whole Foods

Minerals have flavor; otherwise you wouldn't hear bottled water companies and water filter products claiming that they add minerals to their products for flavor. You can taste flavor differences in water based on the different minerals added. This is a fact. The same is true with food. Salt, sugar, grains, and other things come to us from nature with vitamins, minerals, fibers, and natural oils intact. Through processing, these are largely stripped out of the final product, which intensifies some flavors or qualities but depletes others.

Whole foods, on the other hand, have all or most of their original vitamins, minerals, fibers, and oils intact. This means that those subtle flavors found in minerals are present, creating a fuller, more comprehensive flavor. It is not possible for refined foods to duplicate these full flavors, which is one reason why home-cooked, whole-food meals taste so much better than manufactured ones, and why whole food gluten-free foods taste so much better than their refined counterparts.

Here are some other benefits of eating whole foods.

1. Whole foods nourish your body, which is a must if you have compromised intestinal health like most people with celiac disease or gluten intolerance. Eating a healthy, whole food diet is absolutely essential to rebuild intestinal and thus overall heath.

2. Eating a diet consisting of mostly whole foods allows you to get those nutrients in a way that your body was designed to get them, through food, so that you will have less of a need for supplements.

3. Whole foods taste better; they're like 3-D movies for your taste buds. You don't realize what you're missing until you try it, but once you do, you can't go back to 2-D.

4. Whole foods increase satiety, enabling you to feel satisfied with less food.

The term "whole foods" doesn't just relate to grains, salt, and sugars. It's the same with eating whole animal products from healthy animals and eating plenty of fresh, in-season produce. All of these contribute to a healthy, well-balanced diet.

Here's a picture of both SuCaNat and sea salt that I keep on my counter. You'll notice the rich molasses color of the sugar and the specs of minerals in the salt.

Secret #2	Sprouting & Souring

The first time I purchased brown rice flour from the health food store, it took only one recipe to know that anything I made from it would taste nasty. This is because it was stale, rancid, and very gritty. I've heard of Authentic Foods's superfine brown rice flour that's specially milled and sweeter in taste than others, but it can be pricey and difficult to find. But I discovered a gluten-free secret that I'm going to share with you as long as you promise not to tell anyone. Sprouting and dehydrating rice and then grinding it into flour = sweet, fine-milled, non-rancid flour. This is because

1. There's something magic about the germination process, especially in rice, that dissolves the rancid, stale flavor that it gets before you even open the bag. Germinated rice is also known as GABA rice because its creation of gamma-aminobutyric acid; a calming neurotransmitter in the brain.

2. Once germinated and then dehydrated, the rice may be ground into fresh flour that has a much better flavor than anything you can buy at the health food store.

3. This flour is much finer than what you can purchase at the store because the sprouting process softens the shell, producing a finer milled product.

The Secrets of Making Gluten-Free Products

In addition to tasting better, sprouting also does wonders for the nutrition of the product.

1. Soaking, sprouting, and cooking neutralizes phytic acid and lectins,[2] natures preservative on grains, nuts, seeds, and beans that can destroy intestinal lining and prevent nutrient absorption.

2. Sprouting increases nutrients and converts starches to vegetable sugars,[3] so you can technically say you're eating veggies for dessert.

Souring

Along with sprouting, souring also does wonders for gluten-free baking and health. This is because

1. Souring neutralizes phytic acid and lectins and helps to predigest grains. It is something cultures all over the world have done for centuries.[4]

2. It creates a lighter, fluffier, tastier product.

3. Souring has a tendency to create a gluey consistency in grains.

How does souring relate to gluten-free baking?

When using gluten-free grains, souring before use decreases graininess and creates a gluey structure so GF products end up less crumbly. It's way worth the effort. When I would sour wheat for pancakes, 24 hours later, I had a stringy, gluey blob of batter that I almost needed scissors to cut into individual pancakes. The same principle applies in the gluten-free world. Take Injera (Ethiopian bread), for example. This bread is made only from souring teff and water for a couple of days, adding salt, and cooking the batter like a pancake. It holds together without xanthan gum or anything else because souring has a tendency to make certain GF grains like teff and certified gluten-free oats gluey.

Souring and sprouting take added effort and planning when cooking, but I've discovered that gluten-free baking in general takes added effort and planning anyway because of the need to think ahead, make special flour blends, and/or make trips to a health food store. This planning and effort are inherent in gluten-free living whether you choose to go the refined starch and gum route or the whole food route. Here are some different options for those not quite ready for the whole sprouting/souring experience.

Option 1: Start with souring and sprouting grains and/or beans. Then cook and store, or cook and dehydrate them to grind into flour when needed. This way, your bean flour won't taste like some kind of lethal poison.

Option 2: Use flours that haven't been soured or sprouted (except for bean, unless you happen to like the flavor of lethal poison.) Using these whole grains will still be much better for you than the refined starchy diet.

Option 3: I haven't thought of a third option, although one could be that if you choose to eat the white, refined GF goodies, you could possibly become a financially challenged diabetic after spending $7.00 for a box of brownie mix consisting of 90% refined starches with next to no fiber.

Section Three

My Gluten-Free Pantry

If you opened my pantry, you would see the following things: a large bag of SuCaNat (dehydrated cane sugar), food storage items like organic canned tomatoes, fresh things like potatoes and onions, my GF oats, and some bottles of experimental grape jelly that look more like thick, chunky grape juice from last year's grape production. First off, you may wonder what in the world that grape stuff is and second, what SuCaNat is and why I would have such a big bag of it. It's sugar with its original nutrients intact, nourishing you and at the same time pleasing your taste buds, and the reason I have such a big bag of it is so I don't have to make a bazillion trips to the nearest health food store to get it. That is just one example of a whole food item that I stock in my house.

While you're still looking in my pantry, I would like to explain what I use in my gluten-free cooking and why I use those things while listing my ratings for them or their pros and cons.

Grains, Binders, Things I Use

Grains

. . . .

GF Oats, rolled  (3 out of 5 stars)

Can be ground into flour. Holds less water than wheat, so you need more of it to equal a cup of wheat flour.

GF Oats, steel cut (4 out of 5 stars)

These get 4 out of 5 stars because it's less processed than rolled oats. Can be soaked and used for breakfast or ground into flour. Something else you can do is soak the grain, drain and rinse, and then dehydrate it to help in the digestion process.

Brown Rice, germinated  (4 out of 5 stars)

It would be a 5 of 5 if it weren't for the little arsenic attribute. Rice has a tendency to grab arsenic from the ground where it's present. Most rice grown in the US is grown in the South, where the arsenic levels are higher. California-grown rice has less. Also, soaking, rinsing, and rinsing, and rinsing, does decrease the amount of arsenic found in the rice grain.

Superfine Brown Rice Flour  (3.5 out of 5 stars)

Great for using in sourdough products but has a more bitter/rancid flavor than sprouted.

Jillayne Clements

Brown Rice Glue Flour  (4.5 out of 5 stars)

Sprouted, cooked, and dehydrated rice flour that adds a super gluey-ness to baked goods. Can be made with regular short grain brown rice or sweet rice (even more gluey.) A drier flour, so you need less liquid when baking, usually. No grit.

Sprouted Sweet Rice Flour  (4.75 out of 5 stars)

Acts similar to the cooked brown rice flour in its sticky ability, only it holds less water, which I like.

Super glue Flour  (4.75 out of 5 stars)

Sprouted and cooked sweet rice flour. It's hard to break this stuff apart; a little bit can bind a lot.

Teff  (4.25 out of 5 stars)

Has a gluey quality when cooked. A bit grainy, but that improves with soaking, dehydrating, and grinding into flour. Comes in a darker color and ivory.

My Gluten-Free Pantry

Nut & Bean Flours

Coconut Flour

Pro(s): High in fiber and nutrients and absorbs a lot of moisture, so less flour is needed in recipes.

Con(s): Has a strong flavor that is hard to disguise.

Almond Flour

Pro(s): Tastes mild, works well for added protein in recipes.

Con(s): Doesn't hold or add structure to recipe alone. (This was another batch of muffins that ended up on the floor of my oven.)

Cashew Flour

Pro(s): Good source of protein, adds bulk to recipes, mild flavor.

Con(s): More expensive.

Beans

White beans, sprouted and cooked

Pro(s): Versatile and has a much more pleasant taste than difficult-to-digest bean flour that is typically used in GF cooking. It can be used in sweet and non-sweet bread recipes.

Con(s): Very moist and dense. Some dry flour like coconut or cocoa or oat flour is needed to create more body when cooking with non-dehydrated cooked beans.

Same pros and cons as white beans. Black beans taste fabulous as the basis for brownies. Especially with chocolate frosting made with real butter, cocoa, and powdered cane sugar.

Leavening Agents

Baking Powder—I use a gluten-free and aluminum-free brand like Rumford. Baking powder is my friend.

Baking Soda—works as a leavening agent when combined with something acidic like sourdough. Great for pancakes and other batters. It also causes cookies to spread.

Egg—Just good, old-fashioned, farm-fresh eggs work great to bind and fluff things up. Farm fresh are best because the hens are allowed to roam and eat bugs, contributing to their nice orange yolks, which are high in vitamin A.

Seeds

Flax—Awesome oil source, great for the digestive system, great egg replacer (only it doesn't whip up to make a meringue like egg whites, which I think is rather sad).

Sesame seeds—Great for making crackers and bars.

Starches

Arrowroot Powder—whole root, not just the starch, although it still is a starch. I use a minimal amount in my cooking. None in my breads.

Non-GMO Cornstarch—I use a minimal amount on rare occasion, like dusting homemade egg roll wraps to keep them from sticking.

Sweeteners

....

SuCaNat or Rapadura—Dehydrated cane sugar, a natural, minimally processed sweetener that contains all of Mother Nature's goodness, like minerals (even chromium to help digest sugar).

Raw Honey—Super yummy sweet syrup made by bees. Despite popular belief, it has many beneficial properties, one of which is combatting or alleviating seasonal allergies.

Agave—Syrup made from the agave plant and is also low glycemic. However, it contains fructose, which may interfere with metabolism in high amounts. Any liquid sweetener may be used in recipes calling for agave.

Coconut Nectar—Syrup tapped from the coconut tree. Very low glycemic, neutral taste. However, it is expensive.

Grade A or B Maple Syrup—Real syrup tapped from maple trees, high in nutrients, rich in flavor.

Oils

....

Butter—Great source of fat when made from healthy, properly fed cows. When this isn't possible, then at least healthy cows that haven't been injected with hormones or medications (because what they eat and are injected with goes through their milk and into you).

Coconut Oil, Virgin or extra virgin—anti microbial, antibacterial, antifungal, helps thyroid function—the best oil to use for cooking because of its high heat tolerance as opposed to most other oils. A great butter substitute whether spreading over toast or using in recipes, and it makes your hands soft if you use it as lotion.

Olive Oil—Great oil for use in salads.

Grains, Binders <small>AND</small> Things I Don't Use
(AT ALL OR VERY MUCH)

Grains

Quinoa  (3 out of 5 stars)

I use quinoa mainly as a breakfast cereal. It has a stronger flavor, so I don't use it in baking that much.

Millet (2.75 out of 5 stars)

Same as quinoa.

Amaranth (1.5 out of 5 stars)

This one gets a 1.5 star rating out of 5 because it tastes like dirt, and though healthy societies of the past were known for throwing a little ash or clay into their food for digestion, I never have acquired such a taste.

Buckwheat (2 out of 5 stars)

The flavor is strong, and the starches don't sit well with me.

Sorghum  (3 out of 5 stars)

It's fine if you don't sprout it, but if you do, CAUTION! Sprouting sorghum creates lethal doses of cyanide. Seriously.

My Gluten-Free Pantry

Gums

. . . .

Xanthan—I don't use this at all. Xanthan gum is made of powdered vegetable sugars fermented by the bacteria *xanthomonas campestris*. Some people do not tolerate it very well, it can have an unpleasant aftertaste, and it can be gummy if you use too much. It's also expensive. My decision not to use it is personal preference.

Guar Gum—Natural, and the only gum I use, though not that often.

Starches

. . . .

Potato Starch—I go to great lengths—like soaking and rinsing—to remove as much starch as possible from my potatoes before using them so that they are extra light and fluffy and have less starch. I don't want to add it back into my diet in bulk.

Tapioca Starch—I don't use this in bread recipes at all because of the blood sugar thing, or as a thickener in things like jams because of its slimy consistency. However, I do use the quick tapioca pearls on occasion to thicken berry pie topping.

Oils

Partially Hydrogenated Oil—For heart health.

Margarine—Because margarine is made primarily of unhealthy oils, it is much better to use butter.

Soybean Oil—or anything soy, for that matter, because of its goitrogenic nature to suppress thyroid,[6] is not a good thing unless you like feeling sluggish, tired, cold, and irritable.

Sweeteners

Refined Sugar—Because of the blood sugar roller coaster thing and a slew of others like suppression of the immune system.

High-Fructose Corn Syrup—Because it interferes with metabolism, it is harder to digest and messes with blood sugar levels.[5]

Xylitol—A sugar alcohol sweetener with less calories and blood sugar altering effects of table sugar. Con(s): Side effects are gas, bloating, and diarrhea; symptoms you may get by eating doses larger than a piece of gum. If you do decide to try out xylitol, just make sure it's okay before you take a long drive to some remote place like Little Sahara Sand Dunes . . . just saying.

Tips to Avoid Accidentally Making Bread Crumbs

Through the experience of creating whole food, gluten-free recipes, I have had more failures than I would like to admit. By trial and error, I have come up with quite a list to make GF baking easier and more successful.

1. Line the bottom of baking pan for cake or bread with parchment paper. That way, your cake comes out in one piece instead of just the top half followed by five minutes of digging out the bottom portion.

2. Roll out dough for crackers and cookie cutouts directly on a buttered and floured, rimless cookie sheet to save transfer time and also to prevent the dough from falling apart on the way there.

3. Roll out dough for cookies or crackers between two sheets of plastic wrap. When you are done, peel off the top layer and use the bottom layer to transfer dough to the baking dish.

4. Time is an ally in GF baking. Letting cookies cool for 10 or so minutes on the cookie sheet before removing them helps them set. Waiting for a loaf of bread to cool before slicing helps it to gel better and helps the flavors to deepen.

5. Save anything that turns to crumbs because they can be reused in various different recipes, unless they're burned garbanzo bean muffin crumbs from the bottom of . . . let's say an oven—those can be tossed.

6. When a recipe calls for souring a batter for 12–24 hours, this helps improve taste. Souring also causes the batter to become gluey, so you can make sourdough pancakes without gluten that don't fall to pieces on the griddle. And because souring dough is also acidic nature, when something alkaline like baking soda is added to it, the two combine chemically to create air bubbles, which add fluff to the final product.

Jillayne Clements

7. When you are making yeast breads and the recipe calls for extra flour for handling, knead in enough flour so that it doesn't stick and so that it can be handled and will hold its shape when baking. It should resemble regular wheat dough in consistency.

8. For best results on yeast breads, sour for 12–24 hours. Most of the time, this does not create a sour taste; rather, it causes the flours to stick together better and rise better.

9. Corn was meant to be treated with lime before use or your tortillas would look like those in the blooper section. Treating corn with lime (nixtamalization) increases its nutrients—especially niacin—neutralizes phytic acid, increases calcium, and softens the husks and makes the end product taste better.[7]

10. Let cream puffs cool in the oven with the door propped open rather than rush them outside in frigid temperatures to your faux kitchen to take a picture of their fluffy loveliness, or they may end up looking like lumpy pancakes. See picture in blooper section.

11. Let flours sit for 15 to 20 minutes to absorb moisture before baking and to reduce graininess.

12. Warn your children before they take a giant mouthful of experimental sourdough bread that it may not be to their liking.

13. When souring dough for a recipe, you may use non-prepared flours (e.g. non-sprouted rice flour) because the souring process properly prepares them. When baking quick breads and cookies or crackers, it is best to use sprouted flours.

14. Flaxseed meal mixed with water can be used as an egg substitute. In most recipes, 1 Tablespoon flax meal + 3 tablespoons water = 1 egg.

15. Coconut oil may be used as a substitute for butter in any recipe.

Do-It-Yourself Ideas

One of my ideas for this cookbook was to give you a set of flour blends that could be used to substitute for wheat in any recipe. However, after getting into the nitty-gritty of the book, I have found that different flours do different things for different occasions. For this reason and others (I like to fresh grind my flour so it doesn't go stale before I use it), I have not made an official all-purpose flour blend. Rather, I share with you a variety of successful flour combinations which are found in every recipe. So here are some combinations that I like and how they work. With this knowledge, I want you, my GF friends, to experiment with your own whole food flour blends, and together we'll spread the word about healthier GF eating. And perhaps after one of your inventions, your youngest child will hug you and tell you you're the "awesomest" chef ever.

Rice blend—2 parts sprouted rice to 1 part sprouted sweet rice flour. This blend is great for cookies, sugar cookie cutouts, or rolling out crackers because it holds together well. It is also drier than wheat, so you would need less of it—¾ cup to 1 cup of wheat. Has more of a white bread feel to it.

Teff blend—1 part teff to one part rice flour. Good for a sourdough starter. Teff can be tough all on its own, but rice lightens it. Both flours hold a little more water than wheat flour.

Oat blend—1 part oat flour, 1½ parts rice flour and ½ part flax meal. Awesome for making bread because it has a gluey consistency that also holds air bubbles. Mix with 1½ parts liquid and sour for 12–24 hours. After this time, other ingredients like yeast or sweetener or oil may be added.

Section Four

The How-tos
Step by Step

Sprouting

In order to sprout most nuts, grains, and beans, they need a good soaking. Here's a quick rundown on sprouting in three steps, give or take one.

1. Rinse grain, beans, or nuts, and then place in a large glass or stainless steel bowl. (I make a batch with several cups at a time.) Fill with filtered water. Water level should be an inch or two above grain level.

2. Set in a warm place for 8–10 hours. (Depends on what you're trying to sprout, but this is a good general rule.)

3. Dump contents into a stainless steel colander and rinse.

4. Leave in a warm place, rinsing twice a day until little tails begin to grow.

Rice is a little different. It doesn't need to go into the colander because it sprouts in lots of water. When I sprout rice, I just keep it in the bowl. The water needs changing twice a day. I do this by pouring out as much of the water as I can without sending the rice down the drain. Swish the rice with more water and pour it out again, repeat a couple of times, and then fill it back up with filtered water to soak for another 12 hours. Brown rice will sprout in a couple of days this way.

Jillayne Clements

Souring

Souring is perhaps the easiest method, and although it takes up to 12–24 hours to sour something, preparing it takes only five minutes or less.

1. Place equal parts flour of choice and water in a glass bowl. You may add a teaspoon of raw apple cider vinegar, whey from yogurt with live cultures, or lemon juice to the water, but it isn't necessary. I've made wonderful bubbly sourdough using only the natural yeast that is present in the air in my kitchen (an oven with the light on works wonders), and it doesn't taste as sour as what I make with apple cider vinegar.

2. Stir.

3. Cover with a damp cloth.

4. Set on counter or in an oven with only the light on.

5. After it has soured (it should be a little bubbly and have a pleasantly sour smell) add remaining ingredients and use as directed.

Making Flours

Once a grain has been sprouted and dehydrated, or sprouted and cooked and dehydrated, it can then be used to make flours. Again, this takes about five minutes a day for a few days in a row. You may do big batches at a time, but if you grind your grain into flour right away, refrigerate it or freeze it to keep it fresh.

Sprouted Flour

1. Rinse and drain sprouted whatever-it-is.

2. Place on a dehydrator tray.

3. Set the dehydrator to about 145°F and turn it on.

4. After 12–24 hours, the item will be dehydrated.

5. Run dehydrated, sprouted grain through a grain mill.

Glue Flour

Preparing glue flours is the same as sprouted flours with one added step.

1. Cook rice after it sprouts and before you dehydrate it. Add twice as much water as rice for brown rice, and one and a half times as much water for sweet rice. Cook covered and over low heat until the water is absorbed into the rice.

2. When finished, spread out onto plastic-lined dehydrator sheets.

3. Dehydrate between 145°F and 150°F for about 24 hours or until completely dry.

4. Break into chunks. You may need a hammer. (JK.) But you may need to pre-crumble them in a good food processor until they are back to grain size so they will run through your grain mill without breaking it. Another option would be to use a powerful processor such as NutriBullet, which can take these chunks and turn them into flour, so there's no need for a grain mill.

5. Run it through a grain mill to make flour.

Bean Flour

Since uncooked bean flours are so unpalatable, cooked bean flours are a much tastier (and less gassy) alternative in baked goods, yet they still provide protein and other nutrients that bean flours are known for.

1. Sprout beans.

2. Rinse and pour beans into a Crock-Pot and add water to about an inch above the beans.

3. Cook on low heat for several hours, about 12, until tender.

4. When finished, drain and rinse.

5. Now you may either

    a. Measure and place in zipper-sealed freezer bags to use in recipes calling for cooked beans, like black bean brownies. I premeasure mine with two cups, since most of my wet bean recipes call for that.

    b. Or dehydrate at 145°F to 150°F for about 24 hours or until completely dry and then run through a grain mill to make flour, or store in a container until ready to grind into flour.

Jillayne Clements

Nixtamal
(Corn treated with lime so your tortillas don't end up in crumbs.)

> 2 cups uncooked corn (I use popcorn)
>
> 5 cups filtered water
>
> ½ Tbsp. pickling lime
> (Pickling lime may be purchased at any grocery store in the canning section.)

Bring water and lime to boil, rinse corn, and add it to boiling water. Boil 10–20 minutes and then remove from heat. Place lid over the pan and let the corn soak in the lime water overnight. In the morning, rinse really, really well—rubbing the kernels in your hands to dissolve the husks.

Now you may either

> a. Place on a dehydrator tray for 24 hours at 145°F or until they are dry and then run through a grain mill to make flour for tortillas.

Or . . .

> b. You can grind them before they are dehydrated in a heavy-duty food processor until it becomes a dough. This works well for cornbread.

Nuts & Nut Milk

Nuts also contain phytic acid to prevent breakdown, and they can be made easier to digest by soaking and dehydrating.

Nuts & Seeds

Almonds are especially delicious when soaked and dehydrated.[8]

1. Place nuts of choice in a glass or stainless steel bowl and cover with water about 2 inches above nut level.

2. Add about 1–2 teaspoons of sea salt and stir.

3. Soak for 12–24 hours.

4. Drain and rinse.

5. Lay out on a dehydrator tray and dehydrate for 24 hours at 145°F.

6. Store and use for recipes calling for nuts.

Nut Milk

You can make your own fresh nut milk at home. Doing so is easy and more economical than buying it at the store.

1. Place about 2 cups of raw almonds or other nuts in a glass or stainless steel bowl with filtered water. Water should be a couple inches above the nuts.

2. Add about 1 teaspoon sea salt.

3. Soak for 24 hours.

4. Drain and rinse.

5. Place nuts in a blender with about 4 cups filtered water.

6. Blend.

7. Strain.

8. Drink or season with a little sea salt and honey.

9. Save the pulp. It may be dehydrated and used in many gluten-free recipes.

Section Five

Recipes

Jillayne Clements

yeast breads

Butterhorn Rolls

Makes: 12 rolls • Prep: 20 minutes

Rest/rise: 12 hours/45 minutes • Bake: 25 minutes at 350°F

Ingredients:

1½ cups oat flour

2 cups brown rice flour

¾ cup flaxseed, ground into meal

1 cup milk

3 eggs

¼ cup butter

¼ cup honey

½ Tbsp. yeast

2 tsp. sea salt

In a glass bowl, stir together the flours, flax meal, milk, and eggs. Mixture should barely stick together to form a ball of dough. Cover with a clean damp towel and let rest overnight in a warm place. (Surprisingly, eggs will not go bad during the souring process; just don't eat the dough.)

In the morning, or after 12 hours, melt the butter and honey together until the butter is just melted; not too hot or it will kill the yeast. Stir yeast into honey butter and let it absorb the liquid for about 5 minutes. Stir in salt and then pour honey butter mixture into dough. Use a mixer to mix the dough until liquid is combined. Dough will be sticky.

Turn out dough onto floured surface, using extra flour for handling. Roll into a large circle, about ½–¾ inch thick. Use a pizza cutter to slice into 12 pie-shaped pieces. Starting on the big end, roll dough to create a butterhorn. Place in a buttered 9x13 glass baking dish and let rise in a warm place for about 45 minutes. Bake for about 25 minutes at 350°F.

Jillayne Clements

Yeast Breads

❧ Breadsticks ❧

Ingredients:

1 cup oat flour

¾ cup teff flour

¾ cup rice flour

½ cup flax meal

1¼ cup water

¼ cup honey

½ Tbsp. yeast

1 tsp. sea salt

1 Tbsp. dehydrated cane sugar

1 Tbsp. milk

3 Tbsp. olive oil

¼ –½ cup oat or teff flour to
use for handling

Mix flours and flax together with water and honey in a glass bowl or mason jar. Let it sour for 1–12 or even 24 hours. The longer it sits, the better for you. After desired amount of time, soften yeast, salt, and cane sugar in warm milk and olive oil. Pour yeast mixture into soaked flour and stir together well with a wooden spoon. Dough will be sticky. Divide dough into 12 balls, using extra flour for handling. Shape each ball into a long, skinny rope and place on buttered cookie sheet. Let rise in a warm place for 35–40 minutes and then bake for 25–30 minutes at 350°F. If desired, sprinkle tops with Parmesan Sprinkles (see page 153) during the last five minutes of baking.

Jillayne Clements

❦Cinnamon Rolls❦

Makes: 8 rolls • Prep: 25 minutes

Rest/Rise: 30 minutes/40 minutes • Bake: 25 minutes at 350°F

Ingredients:

1½ cups oat flour

2 cups sprouted rice flour

¾ cup golden flax, ground into meal

2 tsp. sea salt

¾ cup butter, melted

½ cup milk

½ cup agave

4 eggs

¾ Tbsp. yeast

2–3 Tbsp. butter, melted

1–2 tsps. cinnamon

2–3 Tbsp. dehydrated cane sugar

½ cup raisins

In a medium to large bowl, mix together dry ingredients. In a separate bowl, stir together melted butter, milk, and agave. Pour into dry ingredients and mix together well. Let mixture sit for 30 minutes to an hour. After this time, crack eggs into a bowl and sprinkle yeast on top. Let it sit for about five minutes and then stir into flour mix. Roll out dough on a floured surface into a large rectangle. Spread melted butter over top and then sprinkle with cinnamon and sugar and raisins. Roll up, seal edges, and cut into rolls. Place in buttered 9x13 glass baking dish. Rise in a warm place, such as the oven with the light on, for about 45 minutes. When done, bake at 350°F for about 25 minutes. Top with honey butter (see page 158).

Yeast Breads

✿English Muffins✿

Makes: about 7 muffins • Prep: 30 minutes

Rest/Rise: 12-24 hours/20-30 minutes • Cook: 30-35 minutes at 325°F

Ingredients:

1 cup oat flour

1½ cups rice flour or 1 cup rice
flour and ½ cup teff

½ cup flax meal

1½ cups water

1 Tbsp. yeast

2 Tbsp. milk

2 Tbsp. butter

2 Tbsp. dehydrated cane sugar

1 tsp. sea salt

Extra flour as needed for
handling: up to ½ to ¾ cup
more

Cornmeal for dusting

Stir together flours, flax, and water and let sit for 12–24 hours in a warm spot. When ready to use, soften yeast in warmed milk, butter, and sugar. Add salt and then pour into dough. Mix thoroughly. Add extra flour as needed to make dough that can be rolled. Roll out into a rectangle or oval. Use a wide-mouth mason jar lid to cut circles for English muffins. Place on a cornmeal-dusted cookie sheet and let rise for 20–30 minutes. After this time, heat a griddle to 325°F. Carefully place risen circles onto griddle and cook for 5 minutes and then flip them to the other side. Keep flipping every 5 minutes until they have been cooking for 30–35 minutes and are cooked all the way through.

Jillayne Clements

Yeast Breads

❧ Honey Oat Bread ❧

Makes: 1 loaf • Prep: 20 minutes

Rest/Rise: 12 hours/1 hour • Bake: 50–55 minutes at 350°F

Ingredients:

1 cup oat flour

1 cup sprouted or non-sprouted brown rice flour

1 cup ivory teff flour

½ cup golden flaxseed, ground into meal

¼ cup honey

1¼ cup water

½ Tbsp. yeast

2 beaten eggs

1½ Tbsp. salt

Mix flours, flax, honey, and water together in a glass bowl. Cover with damp cloth and leave in a warm place for 12–24 hours. When ready to bake, soften yeast in eggs, stir in salt. Mix well with the dough and spread into parchment-lined loaf pan. Let rise for about 1 hour and bake for 50–55 minutes at 350°F.

Jillayne Clements

❧ Multigrain Bread ❧

Makes: 1 loaf • Prep: 12-24 hours

Rest/Rise: 12-24 hours/1 1/2 hours • Bake: 1 hour at 350°F

Ingredients:

2½ cups oat flour

1 cup ivory teff flour

1 cup brown rice flour

½ cup flaxseed ground into meal

2 cups water

½ Tbsp. yeast

2 eggs

2 Tbsps. honey

2 Tbsps. olive oil

2 tsps. sea salt

In a glass bowl, stir together flours, flax, and water. Stir together until it forms dough. Cover with a damp cloth and set in a warm place for 12–24 hours. After this time, soften yeast in eggs, honey, and oil. Stir in salt, and then pour into dough. Form into loaf, using extra flour if needed to prevent sticking and to hold shape. Should not be sticky, but not dry either, and should hold its shape. Rise for about an hour and a half, and then bake for 1 hour at 350°F.

Yeast Breads

Jillayne Clements

French Bread

Makes: 1 loaf • Prep: 20 minutes

Rest/Rise: 12-24 hours/35-45 minutes • Bake: 45 minutes at 350°F

Ingredients:

1 cup oat flour

1½ cups brown rice flour

½ cup flaxseed ground into meal

1½ cups water

½ Tbsp. yeast

1 Tbsp. honey

1 Tbsp. olive oil

1 Tbsp. water

2 tsp. sea salt

Extra flour of choice as needed to incorporate into dough so that it will hold its shape and for handling: about ¼-¾ cup

1 egg white for wash

Sesame seeds

In a bowl, mix flours, flax, and water and cover with a damp cloth. Set aside for 12–24 hours. After this time, soften yeast in honey, oil, and water. After yeast is softened, stir in the salt and then pour the mixture into the soured dough. Mix well. Then, using extra flour for handling, shape dough into French bread loaf and place on a buttered cookie sheet. Brush the top of loaf with egg white, cut three diagonal gashes along the top, and then sprinkle with sesame seeds. Rise for 35–45 minutes and then bake for 45 minutes in a 350°F oven.

Hamburger Buns

Makes: about 7 buns • Prep: 30 minutes

Rest/Rise: 12-24 hours/30 minutes • Bake: 25-30 minutes at 350°F

Ingredients:

1 cup oat flour

1½ cup rice flour

½ cup flax meal

1½ cups water

1 Tbsp. yeast

2 Tbsp. milk

2 Tbsp. butter

2 Tbsp. dehydrated cane sugar

1½ tsp. sea salt

Extra flour as needed for
 handling: up to ½–¾ cup more

Sesame seeds (optional)

Stir together flours, flax meal, and water and let sit for 12–24 hours in a warm spot. When ready to use, soften yeast in warmed milk, butter, and sugar. Add salt and then pour into dough. Mix thoroughly. Add extra flour as needed to make dough that can be rolled. Roll out into a rectangle or oval. Use a wide-mouth mason jar lid to cut circles for buns. Sprinkle with sesame seeds if desired. Place on a floured cookie sheet and let rise for about 30 minutes; then, bake for 25–30 minutes at 350°F until golden. Dough may also be shaped into hot dog buns.

Jillayne Clements

❦ Bagels ❦

Makes: 6 bagels • Prep: 1 hour 10 minutes

Bake: 35 minutes at 375°F

Ingredients:

2 cups water, divided

½ cup finely ground golden
flaxseed

1 cup oat flour

1½ cups brown rice flour

½ cup coconut flour

1 tsp. sea salt

1 Tbsp. dehydrated cane sugar
or honey

1 Tbsp. yeast

Extra brown rice flour as needed,
up to ½–¾ cup more

6 cups water

¼ tsp. baking soda or 1 Tbsp.
dehydrated cane sugar

In a pan, bring 1½ cups water to boil. In the meantime, grind ½ cup flaxseed into fine meal and pour into a glass bowl. In a separate bowl, mix together flours and salt. When the water comes to a boil, pour over ground flax seed and stir to make a slurry. Stir in remaining ½ cup water, dehydrated cane sugar, and yeast. Let yeast soften and then pour into flour mix.

Stir well until a ball dough forms. Separate into 6 balls and dust generously with brown rice flour to prevent sticking and to prevent the inside from getting soggy while boiling. Shape into bagels, leaving about a 1½-inch hole in the center, and let rise on a cookie sheet for 20 minutes.

While the dough is rising, bring about 6 cups of water to a boil with ¼ teaspoon baking soda or 1 tablespoon dehydrated cane sugar, in a large pan. Boil bagels for three minutes on each side. Drain for a few minutes on paper towels and then transfer to buttered cookie sheet. Bake for 35 minutes at 375°F.

Yeast Breads

Jillayne Clements

❦ Artisan Bread ❦

Makes: 2 loaves • Prep: 15 minutes

Rest/Rise: 1–12 hours/30 minutes • Bake: 40–45 minutes at 450°F

Ingredients:

1 cup oat flour

1¼ cup sprouted brown rice flour

¼ cup cooked sweet rice flour

½ cup flax, ground into meal

1½ cups water

¾ Tbsp. kosher salt

½ Tbsp. yeast

¼ cup warm water

Extra flour to strengthen dough and for handling (up to ½–¾ cup)

Mix together the flours, flax meal, and 1½ cups water. Let rest for a long time: at least 1–12 hours or more. The longer the rest, the better the end product will be. After this time, dissolve salt and soften yeast in ¼ cup warm water. Mix into dough until incorporated. Dough will be sticky, so add more flour, kneading it in a little at a time until it doesn't stick anymore but is still pliable.

Divide dough into two balls, using extra flour for handling. Spread the tops of the balls smooth while placing the extra dough underneath, keeping the underside slightly hollow. Place balls on a well-floured pizza board and cut ¼-inch slashes in the tops. Let rise for about 30 minutes. In the meantime, preheat a pizza stone in the oven to 450°F. When bread is done rising and the oven is hot, gently shake the loaves onto the hot pizza stone. Bake for 40–45 minutes or until the outside is golden but the inside is still moist.

Note: See Blooper #7 to know what happens to artisan bread when not enough flour is in your loaf.

Yeast Breads

Focaccia (Italian Bread)

Makes: 2- 9-10 inch pans   •   Prep: 15 minutes

Rest/Rise: 1-12 hours/30 minutes   •   Bake: 18 minutes at 400°F

Ingredients:

1 cup oat flour

1¼ cup sprouted brown rice flour

¼ cup cooked sweet rice flour

½ cup flax ground into meal

1½ cups water

¾ Tbsp. kosher salt

½ Tbsp. yeast

¼ cup warm water

⅓ cup olive oil

Mix together the flours, flax meal, and 1½ cups water. Let rest for a long time, at least 1–12 hours or more. The longer the rest, the better the end product will be. After this time, dissolve salt and soften yeast in ¼ cup warm water. Mix into dough until incorporated. Dough will be sticky. Divide dough into two balls. Drizzle about half of the olive oil into the bottoms of 2 9- or 10-inch baking pans. Press dough balls into the two pans, using the remaining olive oil to drizzle over the tops to prevent sticking. Press knuckles or fingertips into the bread to create divots. Let rise for 30 minutes in a warm place and then bake for 18 minutes in a 400°F oven. Top with Parmesan Sprinkles (see page 153), Italian seasonings, or even use as a pizza crust.

Jillayne Clements

❧ Scones ❧

Makes: about 14-18 scones   •   Prep: 30 minutes

Rest: 12-24 hours   •   Cook: 12-15 minutes over medium to medium-high heat

Ingredients:

1 cup oat flour

1½ cup rice flour

½ cup flax meal

1½ cups water

1 Tbsp. yeast

2 Tbsp. milk, warmed

2 Tbsp. butter, melted

2 Tbsp. dehydrated cane sugar

1½ tsp. sea salt

Extra flour as needed for handling,
   up to ½–¾ cup more

Coconut oil

Stir together flours, flax, and water and let sit for 12–24 hours in a warm spot. When ready to use, soften yeast in warmed milk, butter, and sugar. Add salt and then pour into dough. Mix thoroughly. Add extra flour as needed to make dough that can be rolled. Roll out into a rectangle or oval and cut with a pizza cutter to make 2- or 3-inch squares. Heat several tablespoons of coconut oil in a pan. Stretch each scone a bit before dropping into hot oil. Cook for 12–15 minutes or until golden and center is cooked. Serve with apricot jam or honey butter (see page 158).

non-yeast breads and wraps

❦Dumplings❦

Makes: 24 dumplings • Prep: 15 minutes

Rest: 12 hours • Cook: 15-20 minutes

Ingredients:

1 cup oat flour

1 cup rice flour

¾ cup milk

1 Tbsp. apple cider vinegar

½ tsp. sea salt

¼ cup olive oil

1 Tbsp. baking powder

2–3 Tbsp. coconut flour

Soak flours, milk, and vinegar together in a covered glass bowl for 7–12 hours. When ready to use, add remaining ingredients. Form into small balls and drop in Vegetable Soup with Dumplings (see page 179). Simmer dumplings in soup about 20 minutes.

Jillayne Clements

Buttermilk Biscuits

Makes: 12 biscuits • Prep: 20 minutes

Bake: 15 minutes at 400°F

Ingredients:

1 cup sprouted brown rice flour

½ cup cooked brown rice flour

1 Tbsp. baking powder

⅓ cup butter

1 cup buttermilk or 1 cup milk
mixed with 1 tsp. raw apple
cider vinegar

In a food processor, mix dry ingredients. Add butter and continue to mix until mixture is crumbly. Add milk until dough forms a ball of dough. Roll dough out on a floured surface and use a lid to a small-mouth mason jar to cut biscuits into circles. Place on cookie sheet and bake for about 15 minutes at 400°F.

Non-Yeast Breads and Wraps

Herb Drop Biscuits

Makes: about 12 biscuits • Prep: 20 minutes

Rest/Rise: 12 hours/45 minutes • Bake: 15 minutes at 400°F

Ingredients:

1 cup sprouted brown rice flour

½ cup cooked brown rice flour

1 Tbsp. baking powder

1 tsp. parsley

½ tsp. onion powder

¼ tsp. garlic powder

⅓ cup butter

1 cup buttermilk or 1 cup milk
    mixed with 1 tsp. raw apple
    cider vinegar

4 Tbsp. water or milk

In a food processor, mix dry ingredients. Add butter and continue to mix until mixture is crumbly. Add milk mixture and extra water until well mixed. Drop dough by heaping spoonfuls onto buttered cookie sheet and bake for about 15 minutes at 400°F.

Jillayne Clements

Crepes

Makes: about 11 crepes • Prep: 10 minutes

Cook: 2-3 minutes per crepe

Ingredients:

¾ cup sprouted brown rice flour

¼ cup cooked sweet rice flour

½ tsp. sea salt

3 eggs

1½ cups milk or ¾ cup milk with
¾ cup water

2 Tbsp. olive oil

In a glass bowl, stir together flours and salt. In a separate bowl, beat eggs, and then stir in milk and olive oil. Pour liquid into flour bowl and stir with a wire whisk until all the lumps are out. Preheat a frying pan over medium to medium-high heat. Lightly butter pan and then pour crepes one at a time by ¼ cup, swirling around in the bottom of the pan. Cook for 1–2 minutes until the top mostly dries. Flip over and cook about 30 seconds on other side. Remove from pan and cool on a plate. Repeat with remaining batter. Serve with sautéed vegetables and Pepper Jack Cheese Sauce (see page 173).

Non-Yeast Breads and Wraps

❧Irish Soda Bread☙

Makes: 1 loaf • Prep: 15 minutes

Rest: 12 hours • Bake: 35-40 minutes at 350°F

Ingredients:

1 cup oat flour

1 cup brown rice flour

⅓ cup flaxseed ground into meal

2 eggs

¾ cup water

2 Tbsp. olive oil

2 Tbsp. honey

1 tsp. sea salt

2 tsp. baking soda

In a glass bowl, stir together flours and flax meal. In a separate bowl, beat eggs and stir in water. Pour into flour mix and stir to form a ball of dough. Cover with a damp cloth and let rest in a warm place for about 12 hours.

After this time, stir together the oil, honey, salt, and soda. Pour into dough and mix until well combined. Use a little flour for handling to shape dough into a ball. Place on a cookie sheet or other baking dish and cut an X in the top of it. Garnish with a little rolled oats if desired. Bake for 35–40 minutes at 350°F.

Jillayne Clements

Non-Yeast Breads and Wraps

Natural Yeast Bread

Makes: 1 loaf • Prep: 15 minutes

Rest/Rise: 12–24 hours/24 hours • Bake: 40 minutes at 350°F

Ingredients:

1 cup oat flour

½ cup sprouted rice flour

½ cup flaxseed ground into meal

1½ cups water

1 Tbsp. kosher salt

¼ cup warm water

1 cup sprouted brown rice flour

Extra flour for handling

Oil for top

Mix together oat flour, sprouted rice flour, flax meal, and 1½ cups water in a mason jar or glass bowl. Let sour 12–24 hours. After this time, dissolve salt in warm water and then stir in the salt water and remaining flour to the soured dough. Form into bread shape (artisan or French bread style), cut slashes on the top, and brush with oil to keep it soft. Cover with a damp cloth and keep in a warm place for about 24 hours. Bake for about 40 minutes at 350°F.

Jillayne Clements

❧Injera (Ethiopian Bread)❧

Makes: 3–4 Injera • Prep: 5 minutes

Rest: 2–3 days • Cook 1–2 minutes on each side

Ingredients:

1 cup dark teff flour

1¼ cups water

¼ tsp. sea salt

butter

Sour teff in water in a covered bowl for 2–3 days or until bubbly. Stir in salt and then preheat frying pan over medium-high heat. Butter pan lightly and then pour batter into pan, cooking for 1–2 minutes or more until the top dries a bit. Flip over. Injera is typically served with different kinds of soups and side dishes (see Bonus Recipes).

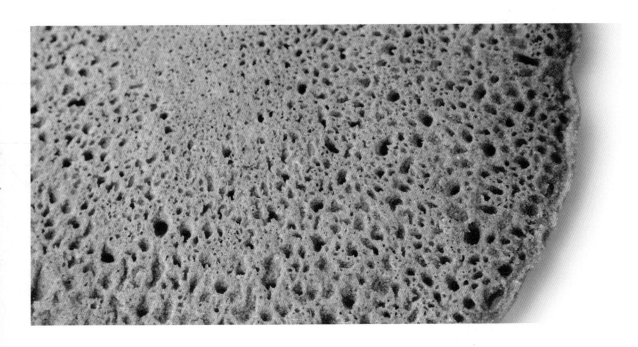

Non-Yeast Breads and Wraps

Jillayne Clements

❧ Cornbread ❧

Makes: 1 9x13 dish (glass) • Prep: 15 minutes

Rest: 12-24 hours • Bake: 30 minutes at 350°F

Ingredients:

1 cup oat flour or teff

1 cup brown rice flour

2 cups water or milk

1 cup nixtamal

3 Tbsp. dehydrated cane sugar

1 tsp. sea salt

1 tsp. baking soda

3 beaten eggs

¼ cup olive oil

Mix oat and rice flours with water or milk and let sour for 12–24 hours. Then stir in the nixtamal, sugar, salt, baking soda, beaten eggs, and olive oil. Pour into a 9x13 baking dish and bake for 30 minutes at 350°F. Serve with Clam Chowder (see page 178).

❧ Cream Puffs ❧

Makes: 12 cream puffs   •   Prep: 25 minutes

Bake: 35 minutes at 375°F

Ingredients:

1 cup water

¼ tsp. sea salt

1 stick butter

1 cup sprouted rice flour

4 eggs

Bring water, salt, and butter to a boil in a saucepan over medium-high heat. When they have reached a boil and the butter is completely melted, dump flour all at once into mix. Remove from heat and stir until dough forms a ball. Cool for 10 minutes. After this time, stir in eggs one at a time until smooth and glossy. Scoop by ¼ cup onto buttered cookie sheet and bake in well-preheated oven at 375°F for 35 minutes. Cool 15 minutes in oven with the oven off and the door slightly ajar. Stuff with Chicken Salad Sandwich Filling (see page 151) or your favorite sandwich or pudding recipe.

Note: See blooper #3 to know what happens if they cool too rapidly.

Jillayne Clements

❧Multigrain Wraps❧

Makes: 4 tortillas • Prep: 15 minutes

Cook: 1–2 minutes

Ingredients:

¼ cup sprouted rice flour

¼ cup oat flour

¼ cup flaxseed ground into meal

¼ cup cooked rice flour

1 tsp. sea salt

¾ cup water

Mix flours, flax meal, and salt together. Add water and let sit for several minutes for flours to absorb water. Divide into 4 balls—use flour for handling. Roll on floured surface until about 5 inches around and then cook on medium-high heat in a pan or griddle for 45–60 seconds on each side.

❧ Tortillas ❧

Makes: 4 tortillas • Prep: 15 minutes

Cook: 1 minute on each side

Ingredients:

¾ cup oat flour

¼ cup cooked sweet rice flour

½ tsp. sea salt

7–8 Tbsp. hot milk or water

Stir together dry ingredients in a bowl. Meanwhile, heat milk or water in a pan over medium heat. When it just begins simmering, pour into flours and stir. All flour should be absorbed into liquid, but it should not be sticky. Divide dough into four balls and then roll out between two flour-dusted plastic sheets. Cook in a pan or on a hot griddle for 1 minute on each side.

Jillayne Clements

Makes: 5-6 tortillas • Prep: 20-25 minutes

Cook: 2-3 minutes

Ingredients:

½ cup water

1 tsp. olive oil

¼ tsp. sea salt

½ cup nixtamal flour

Bring water, oil, and salt to a boil in a saucepan. Pour nixtamal in all at once and stir until it forms a ball of dough. If a little more water is needed, add a little more, 1 tablespoon at a time, until it forms a ball. If it is too wet, you may add a little more nixtamal flour. Working quickly, divide the dough into 5 or 6 balls. Place a ball between two sheets of plastic wrap and press down on the top of it with a plate. Remove top layer of plastic and place tortilla in hot skillet. Cook about 1 minute before flipping to the other side. Cool on a plate. Repeat with remaining dough balls.

pancakes AND cereals

Sesame Seed Granola

Makes: about 3 cups • Prep: 10 minutes

Dehydrate Time: 8-12 hours

Ingredients:

1 cup brown sesame seeds

⅓ cup black sesame seeds

⅔ cup flaxseeds

⅓ cup liquid sweetener

⅔ cup chopped almonds

1 tsp. vanilla

⅛ tsp. sea salt

¼ tsp. cinnamon

fresh fruit and nut milk to top

In a bowl, measure all ingredients except fruit and nut milk and then stir together until well combined. Spread on a dehydrator sheet. Dehydrate 8–12 hours at 115°F. After this time, break granola and divide into bowls and top with fresh fruit and nut milk. Remaining granola may be stored in an airtight container for a couple of weeks.

Jillayne Clements

Makes: about 8 servings • Prep: 30 minutes

Bake: 65 minutes (total) at 400°F

Ingredients:

1¼ cups oat flour

¾ cup brown rice flour

1 cup almond milk or water

1 Tbsp. apple cider vinegar

3 Tbsp. coconut oil

dehydrated cane sugar for
   sprinkling

3 large apples, washed and
   sliced thin

⅓ cup dehydrated cane sugar

1 tsp. cinnamon

6 eggs

1 tsp. sea salt

1 tsp. baking soda

2 Tbsp. dehydrated cane sugar

Mix flours, milk, and vinegar in a glass bowl. Let sit on counter overnight, covered with damp cloth. In the morning, melt the coconut oil in the bottom and sides of a Dutch oven. When melted, sprinkle with cane sugar and cinnamon. Place sliced apples along bottom of Dutch oven, put lid in place, and bake for twenty minutes at 400°F. Meanwhile, stir in eggs, sea salt, soda, and remaining 2 tablespoons of cane sugar to finish the batter. Pour batter over baked apples and cook an additional 45 minutes or until golden. Top with Honey Butter with Cinnamon (see page 158) or eat plain.

Pancakes and Cereals

Jillayne Clements

❧ Sourdough Pancakes ❧

Makes: 18–20 pancakes • Prep: 30 minutes

Soak Time: Overnight

Ingredients:

1½ cups oat flour

1½ cups brown rice flour

1¾–2 cups water

1 Tbsp. apple cider vinegar

2 eggs

1 tsp. sea salt

2 Tbsp. olive oil

1½ tsp. baking soda

Stir together flours, water, and vinegar in a glass bowl. Set on the counter or in oven with only the light on overnight or for 24 hours at the most. Dough should be bubbly, especially inside. In a separate bowl, beat the eggs, salt, olive oil, and baking soda. Stir into batter. Batter should be fluffy. Pour onto buttered griddle set at medium-high heat and flip when bubbles pop and leave holes. Serve with grade B maple syrup, applesauce, or Blueberry Sauce (see page 161).

❧Buttermilk Waffles☙

Makes: 12-13 waffles • Prep: 10 minutes

Rest: 12-24 hours • Cook: 4-5 minutes in waffle maker

Ingredients:

1½ cups brown rice flour

1½ cups ivory teff flour

3 cups milk

1 Tbsp. raw apple cider vinegar

2 eggs

1 tsp. sea salt

2 tsp. baking soda

In a glass bowl, stir together flours and then pour in milk and vinegar. Stir to form batter and then cover with a damp cloth and set aside in a warm place for 12–24 hours. After this time, stir in remaining ingredients and cook in a waffle maker. Serve with grade B maple syrup, applesauce, or Blueberry Sauce (see page 161).

Jillayne Clements

Pancakes and Cereals

Jillayne Clements

❧ Grape Nuts Cereal ❧

Makes: about 4 cups • Prep: 30 minutes • Rest: 12–24 hours

Pre-bake: 25 minutes at 375°F • Bake: 40–45 minutes at 300°F

Ingredients:

1½ cups sprouted rice flour

1½ cups ivory teff flour

2 cups milk

½ cup honey or dehydrated cane sugar

¼ cup coconut oil, melted

1 Tbsp. molasses

1 tsp. sea salt

1 tsp. baking soda

Mix flours and milk together in a bowl. Cover with a damp cloth and set aside in a warm place for 12–24 hours. When you are ready to bake, stir in remaining ingredients.

Divide batter between two buttered 9x13 glass baking dishes. Bake for 25 minutes at 375°F. When done, remove from oven and cut both cakes into chunks. Place as many chunks as will fit into a food processor and pulse until they turn to crumbs. Repeat with any remaining cake portions.

Divide crumbs evenly between the two 9x13 dishes used for baking the cakes and bake again, this time reducing the heat to 300°F and baking for 40–45 minutes or more until the crumbs are crunchy. Cool and store in a container for a quick breakfast.

❧ Apples & Cinnamon Steel Cut Oats ☙

Makes: about 5 cups • Prep: 15 minutes

Cook: 15-20 minutes on low heat

Ingredients:

2 cups steel cut oats, rinsed

5 cups filtered water

a few dashes of sea salt

1 apple, chopped

1 tsp. cinnamon

honey and milk, to serve

Soak oats in water in a stainless steel saucepan overnight. In the morning, stir in a few dashes of salt and bring to a boil. Stir in chopped apples and cinnamon. Cover and reduce heat to low to simmer until oats are soft and apples tender. Serve with a little honey and milk.

Jillayne Clements

Makes: about 6 cups • Prep: 10 minutes

Cook: 10-20 minutes

Ingredients:

½ cup steel-cut oats

½ cup millet

½ cup quinoa

5 cups filtered water

¼ tsp. sea salt

butter, honey, fresh fruit, to serve

Rinse grains and place them in a stainless steel saucepan with water. Soak overnight. In the morning, bring to a boil with the salt. Reduce to a simmer and cook until thick and creamy. Serve with butter, honey, and fresh fruit.

❧ Cream of Rice ❧

Makes: about 5 cups • Prep: 10 minutes

Cook: 10-20 minutes

Ingredients:

1 cup sprouted and dehydrated rice, coarsely ground

4 cups filtered water

¼ tsp. sea salt

a little butter or coconut oil

honey, to serve

Run rice through a coffee grinder or hand mill on coarse setting. Pour into a stainless steel saucepan and fill with 4 cups water. Soak overnight. In the morning, add salt and bring to a boil. Reduce heat and simmer until rice is tender and cereal is thick and creamy. Serve with a little butter or coconut oil and honey.

Jillayne Clements

⟨Danish Cereal⟩

Makes: about 7 cups • Time: 20 minutes

Ingredients:

6 cups almond milk
  or 4 cups almond milk
  + 2 cups water

½ tsp. sea salt

1½ cups sprouted rice flour

1 medium egg

cinnamon and nutmeg

In a large saucepan, bring milk and salt to a boil. In the meantime, stir together flour and egg in a separate bowl. Mix should be lumpy. When milk has come to a boil, stir in the flour/egg mixture. Cook until thick and bubbly and then 1 to 2 minutes more. Remove from heat, serve with a little honey, and sprinkle with cinnamon and nutmeg.

Swiss Oatmeal

Makes: about 4 cups   •   Prep: 20 minutes

Rest: 12 hours or overnight

Ingredients:

1 cup Greek yogurt

1 cup water

2 cups rolled oats

1 tsp. cinnamon

fresh fruit

nuts

honey to taste

In a glass bowl, mix yogurt with water and stir in rolled oats. Cover and let soak overnight on the counter. In the morning, add cinnamon, fresh fruit, nuts, and a little honey to sweeten. As long as you're using yogurt with live cultures, soaking on the counter overnight won't generate harmful bacteria. However, you may choose to place the oat/yogurt mix in the refrigerator overnight.

Jillayne Clements

sweet breads and muffins

Jillayne Clements

Blueberry Muffins

Ingredients:

2 cups white beans
(sprouted and cooked)

4 eggs

¾ cup dehydrated cane sugar

1 tsp. sea salt

1 tsp. baking soda

1 tsp. vanilla

½ cup butter (melted)

2 cups oat flour

1½ cups frozen blueberries

In a food processor or blender, blend beans and eggs until smooth. Add dehydrated cane sugar, salt, baking soda, vanilla, and melted butter. Pour in oat flour and mix well. Stir in frozen blueberries until mixed together. Scoop into 24 oiled muffin tins and bake for 25 minutes at 400°F.

❧ Zucchini Muffins ❧

Makes: 2 dozen muffins • Prep: 20 minutes

Bake: 25 minutes at 350°F

Ingredients:

2 cups sprouted and cooked
white beans (rinsed and drained)

6 eggs

2½ cups oat flour

½ cup sprouted sweet rice flour

1 tsp. cinnamon

1 tsp. sea salt

1 tsp. baking soda

1½ cups dehydrated cane sugar

⅔ cup melted butter
or coconut oil

2 cups zucchini, grated

In a food processor, blend beans and eggs until smooth. Mix in flours, cinnamon, salt, baking soda, and sugar. Pour in melted butter while running and then stir in zucchini last. Pour into buttered or paper-lined muffin tins and bake for 25 minutes at 350°F.

Jillayne Clements

Makes: 2 loaves or 24 muffins • Prep: 20 minutes

Bake: 25-30 minutes (muffins) or 50-55 minutes (bread) at 350°F

Ingredients:

½ cup butter

½ cup coconut oil

1½ cups dehydrated cane sugar

4 eggs

3 cups oat flour

½ cup sprouted rice flour

½ cup sweet rice flour

1 tsp. baking powder

1 tsp. sea salt

1 tsp. cinnamon

¼ tsp. nutmeg

4 ripe bananas

1 cup raisins (optional)

1 cup coarsely chopped almonds (soaked and dehydrated)

In a mixer, cream butter, coconut oil, and sugar. Mix in eggs, one at a time. In a separate bowl, stir together flours and other dry ingredients. In another bowl, mash bananas. Alternate between pouring dry ingredients and bananas into butter mix. Last, stir in raisins and nuts. If making loaves, line bottom of loaf pans with parchment paper, divide batter in half, and pour into pans. Bake at 350°F for 50–55 minutes. For muffins, pour batter into buttered or paper-lined muffin tins and bake at 350°F for 25–30 minutes.

Poppy Seed Bread with Orange Glaze

Makes: 1 loaf • Prep: 20 minutes

Bake: 1 hour at 350°F

Ingredients:

1 cup butter

1 cup dehydrated cane sugar

4 eggs

1 tsp. vanilla

1 tsp. almond extract

¾ cup sprouted brown rice flour

¾ cup sweet rice flour

2 Tbsp. cooked sweet rice flour

1 tsp. sea salt

2 tsp. baking powder

3 Tbsp. poppy seeds

Cream together butter and sugar in a mixer and then add eggs one at a time. Mix in vanilla and almond extract. Mix well. In a separate bowl, stir together flours, salt, baking powder, and poppy seeds. Incorporate the flours into the butter and sugar mixture and then pour the batter into a parchment-lined loaf pan and bake for one hour at 350°F. Top with Orange Glaze (see page 156).

Jillayne Clements

Makes: 2 loaves or 24 muffins   •   Prep: 20 minutes

Bake: 35 minutes (muffins) or 1 hour (bread) at 350°F

Ingredients:

1 cup butter

½ cup dehydrated cane sugar

4 eggs

1 tsp. vanilla

1 (15-oz.) can pumpkin

1 cup sprouted brown rice flour

½ cup teff flour

⅓ cup cooked bean flour

¼ cup cooked sweet rice flour

1 tsp. sea salt

2 tsp. baking powder

2 tsp. cinnamon or nutmeg

¼ tsp. clove

1 cup milk

1 cup chocolate chips

Cream butter and sugar together and then add eggs one at a time. Stir in vanilla and pumpkin. In a bowl, mix together flours, salt, baking powder, and spices. Pour flour mixture into batter and blend, adding milk a little at a time until smooth. Finally, pour in chocolate chips. Pour into 2 parchment-lined loaf pans and bake for about an hour at 350°F for bread or 35 minutes for muffins.

Orange Cranberry Bread

Makes: 1 loaf • Prep: 20 minutes

Bake: about 50 minutes at 350°F

Ingredients:

¼ cup oat flour

¾ cup teff flour

⅓ cup cooked rice flour

¾ cup dehydrated cane sugar

½ tsp. salt

2 tsp. baking powder

¼ cup butter

4 eggs

½ cup orange juice

2–4 tsps. finely grated orange rind

1 cup dried, fruit juice-sweetened cranberries

Mix flours, sugar, salt, and baking powder in food processor. Add in butter and mix until crumbly. Mix eggs and juice together in a separate bowl and pour into dry mixture. Stir in orange rind and cranberries. Pour into parchment-lined loaf pan and bake for 50 minutes at 350°F.

Jillayne Clements

Sweet Breads and Muffins

❧ Applesauce Bread or Muffins ❧

Makes: 2 loaves or 24 muffins • Prep: 20 minutes

Bake: 25-30 minutes (muffins) or 55 minutes (bread) at 350°F

Ingredients:

1 cup butter

1½ cups dehydrated cane sugar

4 eggs

2 tsp. baking powder

1 tsp. sea salt

1 tsp. cinnamon

2 cups steamed and mashed apples with skins

3 cups oat flour

½ cup sprouted rice flour

½ cup sweet rice flour

1 cup raisins

1 cup coarsely chopped, soaked, and dehydrated almonds

Cream butter and sugar in a mixer and add eggs one at a time, scraping the sides as necessary. In a separate bowl, stir together dry ingredients. Alternate mixing into the batter the mashed apples and flour. Add raisins and nuts last. Pour into buttered muffin tins or 2 loaf pans. Bake for 25–30 minutes at 350°F or 55 minutes at 350°F.

Jillayne Clements

❧ Cherry Chocolate Chip Bread ❧

Makes: One loaf • Prep: 20 minutes

Bake: 50-55 minutes at 350°F

Ingredients:

2 cups sprouted and cooked
white beans

4 eggs

1½ cups dehydrated cane sugar

2 cups oat flour

2 Tbsp. cooked sweet rice flour

2 tsp. baking powder

½ cup butter, melted

1 tsp. almond extract

2 cups frozen cherries

1 cup mini chocolate chips
(Enjoy Life is a good brand)

In a food processor, blend beans and eggs until smooth. Add sugar to the beans and eggs and continue to blend. In a separate bowl, mix the flours and baking powder together and then mix in with the egg and bean batter. Batter will be somewhat thick. Pour melted butter and almond extract into the batter while the food processor is still running. Batter will thin out a bit. Add in the cherries and chocolate chips last, and only mix briefly so they don't get chopped into tiny pieces. Place parchment paper in the bottom of a large loaf pan and pour batter on top. Bake in a 350°F oven for 50–55 minutes or until a toothpick in the center comes out clean. Cool a bit before slicing.

Sweet Breads and Muffins

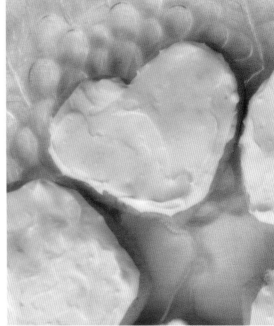

cookies

Jillayne Clements

❧Oatmeal Raisin Cookies☙

Makes: about 40 cookies   •   Prep: 20 minutes

Bake: 10 minutes at 375°F

Ingredients:

¾ cup butter or coconut oil

1½ cups dehydrated cane sugar

1 egg

1 tsp. vanilla

1¼ cups rolled oats

1 cup oat flour

½ cup ivory teff flour

¼ tsp. baking soda

½ tsp. sea salt

1 tsp. cinnamon

1 cup raisins

Mix butter and sugar until light and fluffy. Add egg and vanilla and mix more until even more light and fluffy. In a separate bowl, stir together oats, flours, baking soda, salt, and cinnamon. Pour into butter mixture and mix until well blended. Stir in raisins and drop by spoonfuls onto cookie sheet. Bake for 10 minutes at 375°F.

Peanut Butter Cookies

Makes: about 2 dozen cookies • Prep: 20 minutes

Bake: 10 minutes at 350°F

Ingredients:

½ cup butter

¾ cup peanut butter

1¼ cup dehydrated cane sugar

1 egg

1 tsp. vanilla

1 cup oat flour

½ cup ivory teff flour

¼ tsp. baking soda

Dehydrated cane suger for rolling

Combine butter and peanut butter in a mixer. Blend in sugar and mix well. Add egg and vanilla and beat until slightly fluffy. In a separate bowl, stir together flours and soda. Pour into peanut butter mix and blend. Roll 1–1½-inch balls between palms and roll in sugar. Place on ungreased cookie sheet and press down with a fork. Bake in a 350°F oven for 10 minutes.

Jillayne Clements

❧Chocolate Coconut Drops❧

Makes: 28 cookies • Prep: 20 minutes

Bake: 8-10 minutes at 375°F

Ingredients:

½ cup butter or coconut oil

½ cup dehydrated cane sugar

1 egg

1 tsp. vanilla

1¾ cup coconut flakes,
  ground into a coarse flour

¼ cup cocoa powder

¼ tsp. sea salt

½ tsp. baking soda

¾ cup semi-sweet mini chocolate
  chips (Enjoy Life brand)

Mix butter or coconut oil and cane sugar until well blended. Add egg and vanilla and mix until light and fluffy. Measure out coconut flakes in a separate bowl. Stir in cocoa powder, salt, and baking soda, and then mix into butter mix. Blend well and then stir in chocolate chips. Roll into 1-inch balls on ungreased cookie sheet, and place them 2–3 inches apart. Bake at 375°F for 8–10 minutes.

White Chocolate Chip Macadamia Nut Cookies

Makes: about 3 dozen cookies   •   Prep: 20 minutes

Bake: 8-10 minutes at 375°F

Ingredients:

1 cup butter

1½ cups dehydrated cane sugar

2 eggs

1 tsp. vanilla

¼ tsp. almond extract

1¼ cup ivory teff flour

1 cup rice flour or 1¼ cups oat flour

1 tsp. sea salt

¼ tsp. baking soda

½ cup macadamia nuts

1–1½ cups white chocolate chips (like Sun Spire brand)

Cream butter and sugar together. Beat in eggs, one at a time, and whip until fluffy. Add vanilla and almond extract. In a separate bowl, stir together dry ingredients. Mix into egg mixture, then stir in nuts and white chocolate chips. Drop by spoonfuls onto cookie sheet. Bake for 8–10 minutes at 375°F. Cool on pan for 10–15 minutes to set.

Jillayne Clements

Cookies

Chocolate Chip Cookies

Makes: about 3 dozen cookies   •   Prep: 15 minutes

Bake: 8–10 minutes at 375°F

Ingredients:

¾ cup butter

1½ cups dehydrated cane sugar

1 egg

1 tsp. vanilla

1¼ cup ivory teff flour

½ cup brown rice flour

1 tsp. arrow root powder

¼ tsp. sea salt

1½ cups semi-sweet mini chocolate chips (like Enjoy Life brand)

In a mixer, cream butter and sugar together. Add egg and vanilla and beat until smooth. In a separate bowl, mix together flours, arrow root, and salt. Stir together well and then pour into mixer. Blend well and then stir in chocolate chips. Drop by spoonfuls onto ungreased cookie sheet. Bake in a 375°F degree oven for 8–10 minutes.

Jillayne Clements

❦ Chocolate Mint Cookies ❦

Makes: 3 dozen cookies • Prep: 20 minutes

Bake: 8–10 minutes at 375°F

Ingredients:

¾ cup butter

1½ cups dehydrated cane sugar

2 eggs

1 tsp. vanilla

1–3 drops of mint essential oil
(therapeutic quality)

1¼ cup oat flour

1 cup teff flour

2 Tbsp. cooked sweet rice flour

¼ cup cocoa or carob powder

½ tsp. sea salt

¼ tsp. baking soda

1½ cups chocolate chips
(mini, mint, white, or a
mix of all)

Cream butter and sugar in a mixer. Add eggs, one at a time, and vanilla and mint oil. Cream until light and fluffy, about 2 minutes. In a separate bowl, stir together dry ingredients and then mix into wet. Add chocolate chips last. Drop onto cookie sheet by spoonfuls and bake for 8–10 minutes at 375°F.

Cookies

Peanut Butter Chocolate Cookies

Makes: about 3 dozen cookies • Prep: 15 minutes

Bake: 10 minutes at 350°F

Ingredients:

½ cup coconut oil

2 Tbsp. butter

1¾–2 cups dehydrated cane sugar

½ cup peanut butter

1 tsp. vanilla

2 eggs

¼ cup cocoa

2 cups sprouted brown rice flour

1 cup unsweetened coconut flakes

¾ tsp. baking soda

¾ tsp. baking powder

⅓ tsp. sea salt

½ bag chocolate chips

Cream coconut oil, butter, and sugar together, along with peanut butter and vanilla. Beat in eggs, one at a time, and mix until fluffy. In a separate bowl, stir together dry ingredients and then add to wet. Stir in chocolate chips and drop by spoonful onto cookie sheet. Bake for 10 minutes at 350°F.

Jillayne Clements

Ginger Snaps or Gingerbread Men

Makes: about 2 dozen cookies • Prep: 20 minutes
Bake: 10-12 minutes at 350°F

Ingredients:

½ cup butter

1 cup dehydrated cane sugar

1 egg

¼ cup molasses

1¼ cup ivory teff flour

¾ cup dark teff flour

½ tsp. sea salt

1½ tsp. ginger

1½ tsp. cinnamon

2 tsp. arrow root powder

Dehydrated cane sugar for
    rolling cookies

Mix butter and dehydrated cane sugar until well combined. Add egg and then whip until creamy. Slowly pour in molasses while mixer is running. In a separate bowl, mix the flours, salt, and seasonings. When the butter/molasses mixture is well combined, pour in mixer, pulsing so flour doesn't fly all over the place, until well mixed. Roll cookies between palms to form a ball and then roll in sugar and place on cookie sheet. Bake for 10–12 minutes at 350°F. For gingerbread men, roll dough into a large rectangle between two plastic sheets, about ¼ inch thick. Cut with floured cookie cutters and transfer to greased cookie sheet. Bake for 8–10 minutes at 350°F.

Cookies

⚬Sugar Cookie Cutouts⚭

Makes: about 1 dozen cookies • Prep: 15 minutes

Chill: 20 minutes • Bake: 6–8 minutes at 375°F

Ingredients:

½ cup butter

½ cup honey

1 egg

½ tsp. vanilla

1 cup sprouted rice flour

½ cup cooked rice flour

¼ tsp. sea salt

½ tsp. baking soda

In a mixer, whip butter and honey together. Add egg. When fluffy and smooth, mix in vanilla. In the meantime, stir together in a separate bowl the flours, salt, and baking soda. Mix flour into honey butter mix. Remove bowl from mixer, cover with a towel or plastic, and refrigerate for about 20 minutes or until dough becomes stiffer.

After dough is chilled, roll dough between two sheets of plastic until about ¼ inch thick. Remove the top layer of plastic, cut cookies with cookie cutters, and then transfer to buttered or floured cookie sheet. Use the bottom layer of plastic to transfer cookie shapes to cookie sheet but flip them upside down and then remove the plastic. (You don't want to bake the plastic with the cookies.) Bake for 6–8 minutes at 375°F.

Jillayne Clements

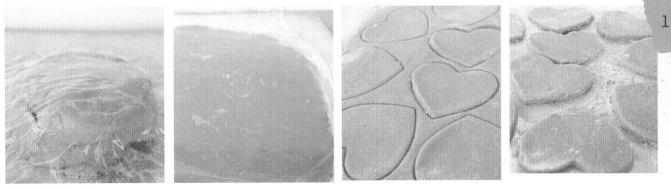

Cookies

❧ Snickerdoodles ❧

Makes: about 2 dozen cookies • Prep: 15 minutes

Bake: 6-8 minutes at 375°F

Ingredients:

½ cup butter

¾ cup dehydrated cane sugar

1 egg

1 tsp. vanilla

½ cup sprouted rice flour

½ cup sweet rice flour

1 Tbsp. cooked sweet rice flour

¼ tsp. sea salt

¼ tsp. baking soda

3 Tbsp. dehydrated cane sugar for rolling

1½ tsps. cinnamon for rolling

Cream butter and ¾ cup sugar together. Add egg and vanilla and whip until light and fluffy. In a bowl, mix together flours, salt, and baking soda. Pour into butter mixture and stir until dough forms. Cover and chill dough for 20–30 minutes for easy handling.

In a small bowl, stir together 3 tablespoons sugar and 1½ teaspoons of cinnamon. When dough is chilled, roll into small balls and cover with the sugar cinnamon mix. Place cookies on cookie sheet, 2–3 inches apart, and bake for 6–8 minutes at 375°F. Cool on cookie sheet for about 10 minutes before removing.

Jillayne Clements

Cookies

crackers

❧ Ritzy Crackers ❧

Makes: about 45 crackers　•　Prep: 30 minutes

Bake: 13–15 minutes at 400°F

Ingredients:

⅔ cup sprouted rice flour

⅓ cup cooked brown rice flour

½ tsp. sea salt

⅓ cup butter

½ tsp. baking powder

2 tsp. dehydrated cane sugar

7–8 Tbsp. water

In a food processor, mix together flours, salt, butter, baking powder, and sugar. Mix until crumbly and then mix in water 1 tablespoon at a time until it forms a ball of dough. Roll out dough between two plastic sheets, with a little flour between the ball of dough and plastic. Roll out into an oval or rectangle about ⅛ inch thick. Use a cookie cutter to cut into small round circles. Transfer circles to a cookie sheet and prick with the blunt end of a toothpick. Bake in an oven preheated to 400°F for about 13 minutes. Keep checking for done crackers on the outside edges. After they brown slightly, remove the crackers from the pan onto a plate or cooling rack and return the others to the oven. Repeat until all are slightly golden and serve with crab dip (see page 169).

Jillayne Clements

❦ Wheat-like Thins ❧

Makes: about 80 crackers • Prep: 30 minutes

Bake: 10–13 minutes at 400°F

Ingredients:

⅔ cup ivory teff flour

⅓ cup cooked rice flour

1 Tbsp. + 1 tsp. dehydrated
   cane sugar

¼ tsp. sea salt

¼ cup butter

6–8 Tbsp. water

In a food processor, mix dry ingredients. Cut in butter and blend until mixture is crumbly. Add water 1 tablespoon at a time until it forms a ball of dough. Roll out dough in a rectangle on a buttered and floured rimless cookie sheet. Get the dough as thin as you can, especially in the middle. When finished, use a floured pizza cutter to cut 1-inch squares out of the dough. Use a toothpick to poke holes into each cracker and then bake for 10–13 minutes at 400°F. Watch carefully for crackers on the edges of the pan because they brown more quickly than those in the center. Remove crackers from the cookie sheet as they turn golden and place them on a plate. Continue baking the rest of the crackers a few minutes, removing crackers that are done, until all are golden and crisp when cool.

Crackers

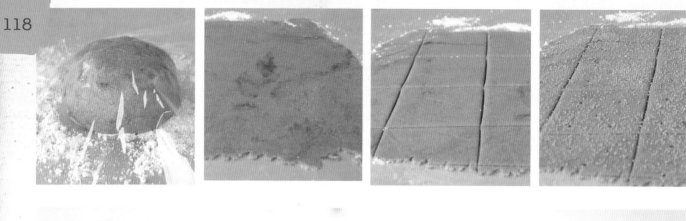

Jillayne Clements

❧Graham Crackers❧

Makes: 12 crackers • Prep: 30 minutes

Bake: 15-18 minutes at 350°F

Ingredients:

½ cup oat flour

½ cup teff flour

½ tsp. baking powder

⅛ tsp. sea salt

3 Tbsp. coconut oil or butter, melted

3 Tbsp. honey

¼ tsp. molasses

1½ Tbsp. dehydrated cane sugar

½ tsp. powdered cinnamon

2 Tbsp. dehydrated cane sugar

Place all but the last two ingredients into a food processor and mix until it forms a ball of dough. Roll out between two flour-dusted plastic sheets. With a pizza or pastry cutter, cut into 2-inch squares. Transfer to a cookie sheet and poke holes in them with the blunt end of a toothpick. If desired, sprinkle the tops with remaining cinnamon and dehydrated cane sugar. Bake at 350°F for 15–18 minutes.

❧ Corn Chips ❧

Ingredients:

½ cup water, more if needed

¼ tsp. sea salt

1 tsp. olive oil

½ cup nixtamal

Bring water, salt, and oil to a boil in a saucepan. Pour in nixtamal all at once and stir until it forms a ball of dough. Drop by tablespoon between two plastic sheets. Press with a plate or use a rolling pin to roll out dough. Cut with a large cookie cutter or the lid of a wide-mouth mason jar. Transfer to buttered cookie sheet and cut into four sections with a pizza cutter. Bake for 12–14 minutes or until lightly golden at 400°F.

Jillayne Clements

Crackers

Poppy Seed Crackers

Makes: 58-60 crackers • Prep: 35 minutes

Bake: 10-12 minutes at 400°F

Ingredients:

⅓ cup teff flour

⅓ cup sprouted rice flour

¼ cup cooked rice flour

1½ Tbsp. poppy seeds

1½ Tbsp. dehydrated cane sugar

¼ tsp. salt

¼ cup butter

6–8 Tbsp. water (enough to form a ball of dough without being too wet).

Place all ingredients but water in a food processor and pulse until crumbly. Add water, one tablespoon at a time, until it forms a ball of dough. Roll between floured plastic sheets. Cut with a cookie cutter and transfer to cookie sheet. Bake at 400°F for 10–12 minutes, remove any golden crackers, and continue baking until the rest are golden. Serve with spinach dip (see page 170).

Jillayne Clements

Sweet Herb Crackers

Makes: about 12 crackers   •   Prep: 20 minutes

Bake: 10-12 minutes at 350°F

Ingredients:

½ cup teff flour

½ cup oat flour

2 Tbsp. water

2 Tbsp. oil

½ tsp. sea salt

2 tsp. dehydrated cane sugar

¼ tsp. onion powder

⅛ tsp. garlic powder

Mix together flours, water, oil, and salt until it forms a ball. Roll out between two floured sheets of plastic and cut with a cookie cutter. Transfer to cookie sheet and sprinkle sugar and herbs over the top. Bake for 10–12 minutes at 350°F.

Crackers

Jillayne Clements

Cheese Crackers

Makes: about 3 cups of crackers • Prep: 35 minutes

Bake: 12-15 minutes at 375°F

Ingredients:

2 cups shredded cheese

¼ cup butter

½ tsp. sea salt

½ cup sprouted rice flour

½ cup cooked rice flour

5 Tbsp. water

Place all ingredients except water in a food processor. Mix until crumbly and then add water 1 tablespoon at a time until it forms a ball of dough. Roll dough onto buttered and floured rimless cookie sheet until about ¼ inch thick. Use a pizza cutter to cut into small squares, about ½ inch. Prick a hole in the center of each cracker and bake for 12–15 minutes at 375°F, removing the edge crackers as they are done and cooking the center crackers until all are golden and crisp.

Crackers

Black Sesame Seed Crackers

Makes: 45 crackers • Prep: 30 minutes

Bake: 10 minutes at 400°F

Ingredients:

¼ cup teff flour

⅓ cup sprouted sweet
rice flour

⅓ cup cooked white
bean flour

¼ tsp. sea salt

¼ cup butter

¼ tsp. onion powder

⅛ tsp. garlic powder

1½ Tbsp. dehydrated
cane sugar

6–8 Tbsp. water

2 Tbsp. black sesame seeds

In a food processor, mix together flours, salt, butter, seasonings, and sugar. Mix until crumbly and then blend in water 1 tablespoon at a time until it forms a ball of dough. Add black seame seeds and pulse until just combined. Roll out dough between two plastic sheets with a little flour between the ball of dough and plastic. Roll out into an oval or rectangle about ⅛ inch thick. Use a cookie cutter to cut into small round circles. Transfer circles to a cookie sheet, and prick with the wide end of a toothpick. Bake in an oven preheated to 400°F for about 13 minutes. Keep checking for done crackers on the outside edges. After they brown slightly, remove them from the pan onto a plate or cooling rack and return the others to the oven. Repeat until all are slightly golden and serve with hot chili (see page 177).

Jillayne Clements

cakes AND desserts

Chocolate Brownies or Cake

Makes: 24 cupcakes or 1 9x13 pan • Prep: 15 minutes

Bake: 40 minutes (dish) or 30 minutes (cupcakes) at 350°F

Ingredients:

2 (15-oz.) cans black beans or 3¼ cups sprouted and cooked black beans

6 eggs

1½ cups dehydrated cane sugar or 1 cup honey

⅔ cup cocoa powder

1 tsp. sea salt

1 tsp. baking soda

2 tsp. vanilla

⅔ cup melted butter or coconut oil

In a food processor or blender, blend beans and eggs until smooth. Add sweetener, cocoa, sea salt, baking soda, and vanilla. In the meantime, melt butter or coconut oil over medium-low heat and then pour into batter while mixing. Pour batter into buttered 9x13 glass baking dish for brownies or divide between 24 paper-lined muffin tins for cupcakes. Frost with Chocolate Frosting (see page 159).

Jillayne Clements

Makes: one 8" round pan • Prep: 20 minutes

Bake: 40–45 minutes at 350°F • Cool: 1 hour upside down

Ingredients:

10 egg whites

1 tsp. lemon juice

1 tsp. vanilla

1 cup liquid sweetener (slightly warm honey or grade B maple syrup)

1 cup sprouted brown rice flour

½ tsp. sea salt

Beat egg whites in a mixer until soft peaks form. Beat in lemon juice and vanilla and then gradually drizzle liquid sweetener and beat until stiff peaks form. In a bowl, stir together flour and salt. Fold flour into mix a couple tablespoons at a time until incorporated. Batter should still be fluffy when finished. Pour into a parchment-lined cake pan and bake for 40–45 minutes at 350°F. When finished baking, invert cake pan over a wire rack. Cool for one hour before removing from pan. Serve with whipped cream and berries. For white cake, double recipe and frost with frosting or cook in a bundt cake pan.

Cakes and Desserts

❧ Yellow Cake ❧

Makes: 1 bundt or 9x13 cake pan   •   Prep: 25 minutes

Bake: 45-55 minutes at 350°F

Ingredients:

⅔ cup sprouted white
    bean flour

⅔ cup sprouted sweet
    rice flour

4 Tbsp. cooked sweet
    rice flour

½ tsp. sea salt

8 eggs, separated

⅔ cup butter, melted

2 tsp. vanilla

1½ cups liquid sweetener

4 tsp. baking powder

powdered dehydrated cane sugar,
    to top

cinnamon, to top

In a bowl, stir together flours and sea salt. In a separate bowl, stir together egg yolks, melted butter, vanilla, and liquid sweetener. Pour into flour mix and set aside for about 15 minutes while the flour is absorbing the liquid. In the meantime, whip the egg whites until stiff peaks form and then fold them gently into the flour mix along with the baking powder. Bake in a buttered bundt cake pan for 30–35 minutes at 350°F. Top with powdered dehydrated cane sugar and cinnamon.

Jillayne Clements

Cakes and Desserts

Fruit Crisp

Makes: one 10-inch round cake pan • Prep: 25 minutes

Bake: 35–40 minutes at 350°F

Ingredients for crisp:

⅓ cup butter

⅓ cup dehydrated cane sugar

⅓ cup teff flour

⅓ cup rolled oats

Ingredients for fruit:

3 cups fruit/berries

¼ cup liquid sweetener

1 Tbsp. sweet rice flour

For the crumb topping, melt together butter and sugar in a saucepan over medium heat. Stir in flour and rolled oats until well blended. Mixture should be crumbly but hold together when pressed. Set aside. Meanwhile, in a separate bowl, stir together the fruit, liquid sweetener, and rice flour. Spread fruit mix into the bottom of a 10-inch, round cake pan, and sprinkle the top of it with crumble topping. Bake for 35–40 minutes at 350°F.

Jillayne Clements

Makes: Two 8-inch round cakes • Prep: 25 minutes

Bake: 30–35 minutes at 350°F

Ingredients:

2 (15-oz.) cans black beans

6 eggs

1½ cups dehydrated cane sugar

1 tsp. sea salt

1 tsp. baking powder

⅔ cup cocoa

½ cup butter, melted

1 recipe for Ice Cream
(see page 155)

1 recipe Hot Fudge Sauce
(see page 162)

In a food processor, blend together beans and eggs until smooth. Add sugar, salt, baking powder, cocoa, and melted butter. Pour into two 8-inch, round cake pans lined with parchment paper. Bake for 30–35 minutes at 350°F. Cool and refrigerate or freeze before placing the ice cream in the center to keep the ice cream from melting into a blob. It helps, too, to make sure the ice cream is very cold before placing between cakes. When the cakes are sufficiently cooled, place one on a plate, scoop the ice cream onto the top of it, and then top with the other cake. Drizzle with Hot Fudge Sauce (see page 162).

❦ Carrot Cake ❧

Makes: 1 9x13 dish • Prep: 30 minutes

Bake: 35-40 minutes at 350°F

Ingredients:

2 cups sprouted and cooked
white beans

4 eggs

2 cups dehydrated cane sugar

2 tsp. baking powder

1 tsp. cinnamon

1½ cups oat flour

½ cup sprouted sweet rice flour

½ cup butter, melted

2 cups finely shredded carrots

1 recipe Cream Cheese Frosting
(see page 154)

In a food processor, blend beans and eggs until smooth. Mix in all dry ingredients and then pour in melted butter. Stir in carrots last. In a buttered 9x13 gladd baking dish, pour batter. Bake at 350°F for 35–40 minutes or until it turns slightly golden and a toothpick inserted into center comes out clean. Cool completely before topping with Cream Cheese Frosting (see page 154).

Jillayne Clements

Makes: about 8 servings • Prep: 15 minutes

Rest: 12 hours • Bake: 1 hour at 350°F in Dutch oven

Ingredients:

2 cups oat flour

1¼ cup brown rice flour

3 eggs

1¾ cup milk

½ cup butter, melted

1¾ cup dehydrated cane sugar

½ tsp. sea salt

2 tsp. vanilla

2 tsp. baking soda

¼ cup butter

¾ cup dehydrated cane sugar

7–8 pineapple rings

In a glass bowl, stir together flours. In a separate bowl, beat eggs and stir in milk. Mix well. Pour wet mixture into flour mixture and stir together. Cover with a damp cloth overnight or for about 12 hours. When ready to bake, preheat Dutch oven (I use mine in my oven set to 350°F). Then stir into the dough mix melted butter, sugar, salt, and vanilla, adding baking soda last. When the Dutch oven is hot, place ¼ cup butter in the bottom until it melts and then sprinkle the remaining dehydrated cane sugar over the top of the butter. Place 7–8 pineapple slices on top of the butter and sugar and spread batter over the top. Return the lid to the Dutch oven and bake for 1 hour at 350°F. You may also cook this in a 9x13 glass baking dish for 40–45 minutes at 350°F in a conventional oven, but you will need only about 6 pineapple slices.

Cakes and Desserts

Jillayne Clements

❧ Fruit Cake Cobbler ❧

Makes: one 9x13 pan • Prep: 15 minutes

Sour: 8-12 hours • Bake: 45-50 minutes at 350°F

Ingredients:

¾ cup oat flour

½ cup sprouted brown rice flour

1 cup milk or almond milk

¼ cup butter

½ cup dehydrated cane sugar

½ tsp. sea salt

1 tsp. cinnamon

1 tsp. baking soda

1 quart bottled fruit with juice,
   or 1 (29-oz.) can fruit with juice

In a glass bowl or mason jar, stir together flours and milk. Let it sit overnight or 8–12 hours. Batter should be bubbly after this time. Right before baking, melt butter in a 9x13 glass baking dish. In the meantime, stir into batter the sugar, salt, cinnamon, and baking soda. Pour into pan over melted butter. Pour fruit, including juice, over the top of batter. Do not stir. Place in preheated oven and cook for 45–50 minutes at 350°F.

❦ German Chocolate Cake ❧

Ingredients:

3½ cups sprouted white beans

6 eggs

1½ cups dehydrated cane sugar

⅔ cup cocoa

1 tsp. baking soda

1 tsp. sea salt

2 tsp. vanilla

⅔ cup melted butter

In a food processor, blend beans and eggs until smooth. Add sugar, cocoa, baking soda, salt, and vanilla. In a pan, melt butter until just melted, and then pour into batter mix while processor is running. Pour into two 8-inch pans lined with parchment paper and then bake at 350°F for 35–40 minutes. Top with German Chocolate Topping (see page 157).

Jillayne Clements

crusts AND things

Dutch Oven Pizza Crust

Makes: 1 medium pizza crust   •   Prep: 30 minutes

Rest: 12-24 hours   •   Bake: 20 minutes at 400°F

Ingredients:

1 cup oat flour

1½ cups sprouted rice flour

½ cup golden flaxseed ground into meal

1½ cups water

½ Tbsp. yeast

2 Tbsp. warm water

1 Tbsp. dehydrated cane sugar

2 tsp. sea salt

In a glass bowl, stir together flours, flax meal, and 1½ cups water. Cover with a damp cloth and set in a warm place for 12–24 hours. After this time, soften yeast in the warm water with the sugar. Stir in salt and pour into dough. Mix until incorporated. Use a little flour of choice for handling. To bake in the Dutch oven, preheat it in 400°F oven. Pour a little oil in the bottom of the Dutch oven, about 2 tablespoons, and spread around. On a well floured pizza board, roll out pizza dough into a small circle. Slide into bottom of Dutch oven and carefully press dough to the sides of the pan. Replace lid and cook for about 20 minutes at 400°F. When done, top with Pizza Sauce (see page 174) and toppings and bake an additional 15–20 minutes.

Jillayne Clements

❧Thin Pizza Crust❧

Makes: 1 medium pizza crust • Prep: 25 minutes

Bake: 20 minutes at 400°F

Ingredients:

¾ cup boiling water

½ cup flax meal

6 Tbsp. olive oil butter

¼ cup honey

1½ tsp. yeast

1½ cups rice flour

¾ tsp. sea salt

In a saucepan, bring water to boil. Add flax meal to boiling water and stir until thick. Mix butter and honey into the flax mix. Butter should melt, and the mix should cool down. When butter is melted, stir in the yeast. Let mixture sit for about five minutes for the yeast to soften. In the meantime, stir together flour and salt in a mixing bowl. Pour softened yeast and flax mix into flour and stir together until it forms a ball of dough. Roll out onto buttered and floured pizza pan. Bake for 15–20 min before adding toppings. Bake an additional 12–15 minutes with toppings.

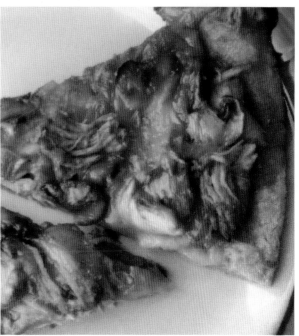

Crusts and Things

Pie Crust, Traditional

Makes: 1 single pie crust • Prep: 20 minutes

Bake: 20-25 minutes at 350°F for pre-baked crust

Ingredients:

¾ cup oat flour

½ cup sprouted rice flour

3 Tbsp. cooked brown rice flour

¼ tsp. sea salt

⅓ cup butter

5–6 Tbsps. cold water

In a mixer, blend together flours and salt. Cut in butter and mix until crumbly. Pour in water one tablespoon at a time until it forms a ball of dough. Roll out between two plastic sheets and then transfer to a pie pan. Bake for 20–25 minutes at 350°F for a prebaked crust, or fill with pie filling and bake according to your favorite recipe's directions.

Jillayne Clements

Makes: enough for 1- 9-inch pie • Prep: 10 minutes

Bake: 25-30 minutes at 350°F

Ingredients:

⅓ cup butter

⅓ cup dehydrated cane sugar

⅔ cup sprouted rice flour

2–4 Tbsp. sprouted sweet
rice flour (mixture should stick
together when pressed)

In a saucepan over medium heat, stir together butter and sugar until the butter is just melted. Stir in flours. Mixture should be crumbly. Press into the bottom of a 9-inch pie pan or use as the crumb topping for one 9-inch pie. For crust, prebake for about 25 minutes at 350°F or until golden. Cool and fill with pie filling of choice. For topping, sprinkle on top of pie filling and bake according to your favorite recipe directions.

Pie Crust, Nut

Ingredients:

- ¾ cup soaked and dehydrated almonds (see how-to section)

- ¾ cup dried coconut flakes (unsweetened)

- 1 cup pitted and chopped dates

- 1 Tbsp. coconut oil, melted

Process almonds, coconut flakes, and dates in a large food processor. While processing, pour in coconut oil until it forms small crumbs. Should stick together when pressed. Press into the bottom of a 8-inch or 9-inch pie pan and chill. Fill with Lavender Berry Cream Pie filling (see page 164).

Jillayne Clements

❧Batter for Frying❧

Makes: about 2½ cups • Prep/Rest: 30 minutes/7–12 hours

Ingredients:

1⅓ cups brown rice flour

¾ cup water

1 Tbsp. apple cider vinegar

1 tsp. sea salt

¼ tsp. pepper

1 Tbsp. olive oil

2 egg yolks

2 egg whites beaten until stiff

Mix flour, water, and vinegar in a glass bowl and let sit at room temperature for 7–12 hours. After 7–12 hours, add remaining ingredients, stirring in whipped egg whites last. Use as a replacement for any breaded recipe.

Bread Crumbs

Makes: ¼ cup • Prep: 5 minutes

Bake: 12-14 minutes at 350°F

Ingredients:

2 Tbsp. teff flour

2 Tbsp. rice flour

½ Tbsp. butter

⅛ tsp. salt

In a small bowl, stir together ingredients until crumbly. Spread on cookie sheet and bake for 12–14 minutes at 350°F or until brown. Another option is to save any crumbly bread experiment and run it through a processor until crumbly and then spread on a cookie sheet and bake until golden and crisp.

Jillayne Clements

Makes: 8 lasagna noodles • Prep: 30 minutes

Ingredients:

1 cup oat flour

1 cup teff flour

4 Tbsp. flaxseed ground into meal

½ tsp. sea salt

2 eggs

6 Tbsp. water

In a bowl, stir together flours, flax meal, and salt. In a separate bowl, beat eggs and stir in water. Pour eggs into flour and stir until a ball is formed. Roll out between flour-dusted plastic sheets. Cut into about 2½ inch strips. Separate each strip and roll to get thinner. For stuffed lasagna (see page 152), place ingredients in center and roll before cooking according to directions. For unstuffed lasagna, cook noodles in boiling water for about 3 minutes and then drain and rinse and use in your favorite lasagna recipe.

❧Won Ton Wraps❧

Makes: 24 wraps • Prep: 35 minutes

Ingredients:

¾ cup sprouted sweet rice flour

¼ cup cooked sweet rice flour

½ tsp. sea salt

1 egg

¼ cup + 2 Tbsp. water

In a small bowl, stir together flours and salt. In a separate bowl, stir together egg and water. Pour into flour and stir until it forms a ball of dough. Roll out onto cornstarch-dusted plastic sheets and cut into circles with a wide-mouth mason jar lid. Lightly dust both sides of each wrap with corn starch to keep them from sticking to each other.

To use, fill with Pot Sticker Filling (see page 150) and then moisten the edges with water to seal them together. Cook in oil for about 15 minutes, rotating to brown on both sides if filled. If just frying the wraps alone, cook for a couple minutes each side and then crumble into salads.

Jillayne Clements

bonus recipes

Pot Sticker Filling

Makes: enough to fill 24 pot stickers • Prep: 15 minutes

Cook: 15–20 minutes at 350°F

Ingredients:

8 oz. sausage

½ cup chopped mushrooms

2 green onions, finely chopped

1–2 tsp. liquid aminos, if desired

In a small bowl, stir together sausage, mushrooms, and onions. May add a teaspoon or two of liquid aminos if desired. Place by teaspoon into center of rolled out Won Ton Wrap (see page 148). Moisten edges of wrap and fold over filling, pressing edges together. Cook on the stove in a little coconut oil between medium to medium-high heat for 15–20 minutes, turning over frequently to prevent the wraps from getting too dark on one side.

Jillayne Clements

Makes: about 8 cups • Prep: 25 minutes

Cook: Chicken Breasts 4–6 hours in a Crock-pot • Chill: 1 hour

Ingredients:

4 chicken breasts,
 slow cooked and shredded

4 stalks celery,
 diced including leaves

2 green onions, diced

⅓ cup sliced olives

½ cup Vegenaise (more/less to taste)

A few dashes each of sea salt,
 onion powder, and garlic
 powder

Shred chicken breasts and dice vegetables. Toss together in a bowl with Vegenaise, season to taste. Chill before serving with wraps, cream puffs, or rolls.

❧ Stuffed Lasagna ❧

Makes: 8 lasagna rolls • Prep: 35 minutes

Bake: 30-35 minutes at 350°F

Ingredients:

1 cup chopped mushrooms

1 onion, chopped

olive oil for sautéing

2 cups chopped fresh spinach

¼ tsp. sea salt

1 (24-oz.) container Greek yogurt

1 recipe pasta (8 freshly made
    uncooked lasagna noodles
    (see page 147)

1 recipe for pasta sauce

1 cup shredded cheese
    (optional)

Sautee mushrooms and onions in a little olive oil until tender and remove from heat. Chop spinach and set aside. Stir together sea salt with the yogurt. Take each lasagna noodle one at a time and spread a bit of the yogurt on it to cover the top. Sprinkle on some chopped spinach and sautéed mushrooms and onions. Starting at one end, roll lasagna noodle up so that it looks like a cinnamon roll only with spinach coming out of it. Place in a 9x13 glass baking dish. Repeat with remaining noodles and filling. When finished, pour pasta sauce over the tops of the rolls and bake for 30–35 minutes at 350°F. Top with cheese during the last 8–10 minutes of baking, if desired.

Jillayne Clements

Parmesan Sprinkles

Makes: ¼ cup • Prep: 3 minutes

Ingredients:

¼ cup Parmesan cheese

½ tsp. garlic powder

½ tsp. parsley

Mix ingredients together in a bowl and sprinkle over tops of buttered breadsticks the last five minutes of baking.

(Pictured with Breadsticks and Focaccia Bread on pages 42 and 54.)

Cream Cheese Frosting

Ingredients:

1 cup butter

2 (8-oz.) pkgs. of cream cheese

½ cup honey

1 tsp. vanilla

In a mixer, whip butter and cream cheese until smooth. Mix in honey and vanilla until smooth. Keep refrigerated.

For pink color, add 1–2 teaspoons beet juice. This can be juice from canned beets.

(Pictured on Carrot Cake and Sugar Cookie Cutouts on pages 134 and 110.)

Jillayne Clements

Makes: about 6 cups   •   Prep: 2 minutes

Process: 20-25 minutes

Ingredients:

4 cups whipping cream

¾ cup dehydrated cane sugar

2 Tbsp. vanilla

Stir together ingredients into a bowl and then pour into an ice cream maker. Follow user directions for time, but generally until ice cream is thick and fluffy.

(Pictured with Chocolate Ice Cream Cake on page 133.)

❧Orange Glaze❧

Ingredients:

2 Tbsp. butter, melted

⅓ cup honey or other liquid
    sweetener

Juice from 1 orange,
    about ⅓ cup

½ tsp. almond extract

½ tsp. vanilla extract

Melt butter in a saucepan and stir in honey or liquid sweetener, orange juice, and extracts. Stir until warm and well blended. Serve over Poppy Seed Bread (see page 92).

Jillayne Clements

❧German Chocolate Topping❧

Makes: enough for one German Chocolate Cake   •   Prep: 15 minutes

Ingredients:

1 (15-oz.) can coconut milk

1 cup dehydrated cane sugar

3 eggs

⅓ coconut oil

dash of sea salt

1 tsp. vanilla

1½ cups dried coconut flakes

¾ cup soaked and dehydrated
cashews or other choice of nut

In a saucepan over medium heat, mix milk, sugar, eggs, coconut oil, and a dash of sea salt. Stir often until mixture comes to a boil. Remove from heat and stir in vanilla, coconut flakes, and nuts.

(Pictured with German Chocolate Cake page 138.)

Honey Butter with Cinnamon

Makes: about 1 cup • Prep: 10 minutes

Ingredients:

½ cup butter

½ cup honey

½ tsp. cinnamon

In a mixer, cream butter and then add honey and cinnamon. Mix until light and fluffy. Serve with Dutch Oven Apple German Pancakes or omit cinnamon and serve with Cornbread (see page 67).

(Pictured with Dutch Oven Apple German Pancakes page 75.)

Jillayne Clements

Chocolate Frosting

Makes: about 2½ cups • Prep: 15 minutes

Ingredients:

½ cup butter

2 cups dehydrated cane sugar, powdered in blender or processor

4 Tbsp. cocoa or carob powder or half of each

3–4 Tbsp. milk

Cream butter, sugar, and cocoa. Mixture will be dry. Add milk, one tablespoon at a time, until smooth and creamy. Spread over cooled cake.

(Pictured with Chocolate Brownies or Cake page 128.)

Yogurt and Granola Parfait

Makes: one serving • Prep: 5 minutes

Ingredients:

½ cup plain yogurt

1 Tbsp. honey

¼ cup strawberries, fresh, washed, and cut

¼ cup blueberries, fresh and washed

1 recipes for Sesame Seed Granola

Mix yogurt and honey together. To make parfait, layer berries with granola and yogurt.

(Pictured with Sesame Seed Granola page 74.)

Jillayne Clements

Blueberry Sauce

Ingredients:

4 cups frozen blueberries

2 tsp. cornstarch

½ cup liquid sweetener or honey

Place frozen berries in a pan with a lid over medium heat until the berries begin to thaw and there is a little juice in the pan. In a glass, stir together cornstarch and 2 teaspoons of the thawed berry juice. (Note: thawed juice should still be relatively cool when mixed with cornstarch or it will turn lumpy.) In the meantime, bring the berries and their juice to a simmer. Pour cornstarch/juice mixture into the simmering berry mixture and stir until it thickens slightly. Mix in liquid sweetener last, and serve over pancakes.

(Pictured with Sourdough Pancakes page 76.)

Hot Fudge Sauce

Makes: about 1 cup • Prep: 5 minutes

Cook: 15-20 minutes

Ingredients:

½ cup butter

3 Tbsp. cocoa powder

½ cup milk

¾ cup dehydrated cane sugar

1 tsp. vanilla

In saucepan over medium-low heat, add butter and cocoa and stir until butter is mostly melted and the cocoa is incorporated. Stir in milk and sugar, waiting for the sugar to dissolve before bringing to a boil. Once dissolved, bring to a boil and boil for about 1 minute. Remove from heat and stir in vanilla. Cool slightly before dishing over ice cream or ice cream cake.

(Pictured with Chocolate Ice Cream Cake page 133.)

Jillayne Clements

Makes: one pie • Prep: 25 minutes

Cook: 12 minutes at 350°F

Ingredients:

one prebaked pie crust

Ingredients for filling:

½–¾ cup honey or other liquid sweetener

¼ cup cornstarch

1 cup milk

3 egg yolks

2 Tbsp. butter

½ cup lemon juice

1 tsp. vanilla

Ingredients for meringue:

3 egg whites

½ cup liquid sweetener

½ tsp. vanilla

Directions for filling:

In a saucepan over medium heat, stir together sweetener, cornstarch, milk, and egg yolks. Stir with a wire whisk often while bringing to a boil. Boil until thick, about 1–2 minutes. Remove from heat and stir in butter, lemon juice, and vanilla. Pour into prebaked pie crust when ready to top with meringue.

Directions for meringue:

Whip egg whites in a bowl or mixer until stiff peaks form. Drizzle in liquid sweetener and vanilla. Should still be relatively stiff. Spread over filling, spreading to the edges of the crust. Bake for about 12 minutes at 350°F until lightly golden.

Lavender Berry Cream Pie

Makes: one pie • Prep: 30 minutes • Chill: 2 hours

Ingredients for filling:

- 1 Tbsp. berry juice
  (from thawing berries)

- 1 (8-oz.) pkg. cream cheese

- ¼ cup Greek yogurt

- ¼ cup agave or other liquid
  sweetener

- ½ tsp. vanilla

- 2 toothpick ends lavender
  essential oil

Ingredients for topping:

- 2 cups (16-oz.) frozen berries
  (combination of blueberries,
  raspberries, blackberries, and
  strawberries)

- Berry juice from the thawed
  berries (approx. ⅓ cup)

- 2 Tbsp. small tapioca pearls

- 2–3 Tbsp. agave or other liquid
  sweetener

(From *The Diet Rebel's Cookbook*)

Directions for filling:

First, begin thawing the berries that will be used for the topping, since their juice is needed for the filling. Meanwhile, mix cream cheese and yogurt until smooth and creamy. Add remaining ingredients one at a time, blending as you go. Dip two toothpick ends into lavender essential oil and swirl around in mixture. (Oil is strong.) Pour filling into chilled nut crust and then return to the fridge while making the topping.

Directions for topping:

Thaw berries in package until berries are mostly but not all the way thawed. Squeeze juice from the bag, about ⅓ cup, and pour into a stainless steel saucepan. Stir tapioca pearls into juice and let sit for 5 minutes before bringing to a boil. When the juice is thick, remove from heat, stir in sweetener, and then stir in berries. Pour over cream filling and refrigerate for a couple hours before eating or freeze for longer storage.

(Pictured with Nut Crust page 144.)

Jillayne Clements

❧ Ranch & Spicy Ranch ❧

Makes: 1 cup • Prep: 7 minutes

Ingredients:

½ cup Vegenaise
(I use Vegenaise made with
grapeseed oil)

⅓ cup Greek yogurt, plain
(Greek Gods is a good,
thick brand)

½ tsp. sea salt

¼ tsp. onion powder

⅛ tsp. garlic powder

1 Tbsp. dehydrated cane sugar

2 tsp. raw apple cider vinegar

1–2 tsp. water, milk, or whey

½ tsp. parsley

In a bowl, stir together Vegenaise and yogurt until creamy. Stir in remaining ingredients. For spicy ranch, omit parsley and add ¼ teaspoon paprika and ⅛ teaspoon red pepper flakes. Serve over salad or use as a pizza sauce and top with cooked chicken and vegetables.

Bonus Recipes

Honey Dijon Dressing

Makes: ⅔ cups • Prep: 5 minutes

Ingredients:

2 Tbsp. Dijon mustard

3 Tbsp. honey

3 Tbsp. plain Greek yogurt

1 Tbsp. olive oil

1 Tbsp. water

1 tsp. vinegar

few dashes of sea salt

Stir the mustard and honey together in a small bowl until smooth. Stir in yogurt and then the remaining ingredients. Chill before serving.

Jillayne Clements

Orange Vinaigrette

Makes: about 1 cup • Prep: 10 minutes

Ingredients:

¼ cup olive oil

¼ cup apple cider vinegar

¼ cup honey

¼ cup juice from orange or mashed fruit, like fresh-squeezed orange juice or mashed raspberries.

few dashes of sea salt

Stir together ingredients in a small bowl. Chill before serving.

Creamy Italian Dressing

Ingredients:

2 Tbsp. plain Greek yogurt

¼ cup olive oil

¼ cup raw apple cider vinegar

½ tsp. sea salt

1½ tsp. oregano

½ tsp. dried basil

2 tsp. honey

In a small bowl, stir together the yogurt with the olive oil and then mix in remaining ingredients. Chill before serving.

Jillayne Clements

❧ Crab Dip ❧

Makes: about 4 cups • Prep: 15 minutes

Ingredients:

3 (8-oz.) pkgs. cream cheese

⅓ cup salsa

¼ tsp. onion powder

⅛ tsp. garlic powder

1–2 green onions, chopped

⅓ cup sliced olives

2 (6-oz.) cans crab meat, drained

In a mixer, stir together cream cheese and salsa. Add remaining ingredients and pulse until stirred together. Serve with vegetables and/or crackers.

(Pictured with Ritzy Crackers on page 116.)

❧ Spinach Artichoke Dip ❧

Makes: about 3 cups • Prep: 10 minutes

Bake: 12–15 minutes at 350°F

Ingredients:

1 (8-oz.) pkg. cream cheese

1 cup thick, plain Greek yogurt

1½ cups finely chopped fresh spinach

1 (14-oz.) can artichoke hearts, drained and finely chopped

½ cup parmesan cheese

¼ tsp. sea salt

¼ tsp. onion powder

⅛ tsp. garlic powder

In a mixer or by hand, blend together cream cheese and Greek yogurt until smooth. Stir in remaining ingredients and then spread into a small glass baking dish (8x11) and bake for 12–15 minutes at 350°F until warm and cheese is melted. Use as a dip for vegetables and crackers.

Jillayne Clements

Taco Seasoning

Makes: enough seasoning for one meal • Prep: 5 minutes

Ingredients:

1½ Tbsp. chili powder

1 Tbsp. dehydrated cane sugar

1 tsp. cumin

1 tsp. sea salt

½ tsp. onion powder

¼ tsp. garlic powder

Stir all ingredients together in a small bowl. Sprinkle over meat and beans while cooking.

(Pictured with Tortilla page 70.)

❧ BBQ Sauce ❧

Makes: about 2½ cups • Prep: 10 minutes

Ingredients:

½ can (15-oz.) tomato sauce

½ cup agave

1 Tbsp. molasses

¼ tsp. sea salt

¼ tsp. onion powder

⅛ tsp. garlic powder

⅛ tsp. pepper

In a small bowl, stir together ingredients. Pour over meat for a slow-cooked marinade.

For pizza, cook 3–4 chicken breasts with sauce in a slow cooker with one sliced red onion. When cooked, shred chicken and pour over precooked pizza crust. Top with shredded cheese and bake an additional 12–15 minutes at 400°F.

(Pictured with Thin Crust Pizza page 141.)

Jillayne Clements

Pepper Jack Cheese Sauce

Makes: about 1½ cups • Prep: 20 minutes

Ingredients:

2 Tbsp. butter

2 Tbsp. sprouted rice flour

1 cup milk

¼ tsp. sea salt

½ cup pepper jack cheese

In a saucepan over medium heat, melt the butter and stir in the flour. Pour in milk and salt and bring to a gentle boil until thick. Remove from heat and stir in cheese. Serve over Crepes (see page 61) or triple the recipe and use for a soup base.

Bonus Recipes

❧ Traditional Pizza Sauce ❧

Makes: about 2 cups • Prep: 5 minutes

Ingredients:

½ can (15-oz.) tomato sauce

½ cup agave

1 Tbsp. molasses

¼ tsp. sea salt

¼ tsp. onion powder

⅛ tsp. garlic powder

⅛ tsp. pepper

Stir ingredients together in a bowl and spread over pizza crust.

Jillayne Clements

❧ Pasta Sauce ❧

Makes: about 2 cups • Prep: 5 minutes

Ingredients:

1 (15-oz.) can tomato sauce

2 Tbsp. dehydrated cane sugar

1–2 Tbsp. liquid sweetener

1 tsp. oregano

½ tsp. sea salt

½ tsp. onion powder

½ tsp. garlic powder

In a bowl, stir together ingredients. Place over stuffed lasagna or other pasta dish.

(Pictured with Stuffed Lasagna page 147.)

Tiny Spicy Chicken Sauce

Makes: about 3¾ cups • Prep: 15 minutes

Cook: 20 minutes

Ingredients:

1 (15-oz.) can tomato sauce

1¼ cup agave or maple syrup
  or other liquid sweetener

⅓ cup dehydrated cane sugar

½ tsp. sea salt

1 Tbsp. molasses

¼ tsp. pepper

about 4 cooked and shredded
  chicken breasts

1 recipe for batter from page 145

In a saucepan, mix together tomato sauce, sweeteners, sugar, salt, molasses, and pepper and bring to a boil over medium heat. Simmer for about 5 minutes and turn off heat. For battered chicken, stir the cooked and shredded chicken into prepared batter. Drop by 1-inch mounds into a little coconut oil (oil will be about ¼ inch in depth) heated in a large frying pan. With a spatula or tongs, turn mounds on all sides for even browning. When golden-brown, place mounds on a paper towel-lined plate to absorb any extra oil. Repeat until all batter and chicken is used. Pour cooked chicken mounds into the warm, prepared sauce, and stir to coat. Serve with rice and stir-fried vegetables.

Jillayne Clements

❧ Chili ❧

Makes: about 6 cups • Prep: 20 minutes

Cook: 25-30 minutes at 350°F

Ingredients:

3–4 chicken breasts, ground

2 cups sprouted and cooked
beans of choice

1 (15-oz.) can tomato sauce

½–1 empty tomato sauce can
of water

1 Tbsp. dehydrated cane sugar

2 tsp. chili powder

1 tsp. sea salt

1 tsp. onion powder

½ tsp. garlic powder

½ tsp. cumin

Brown ground chicken breasts in a pan until cooked. Stir in beans, tomato sauce, and water, and then add seasonings. Simmer over medium-low heat for about 20 minutes for flavors to incorporate. Serve with Black Sesame Seed Crackers (see page 126).

Bonus Recipes

Clam Chowder

Makes: about 6 cups   •   Prep/Cook: 45 minutes

Ingredients:

4 cups milk, divided

1–1¼ cups clam juice (from clams)

½ tsp. salt

2 large potatoes cut into
   small squares (about 3 cups)

4 celery stalks cut into small
   squares (about 1¾ cup)

½ onion, chopped

½ cup sorghum or sprouted
   brown rice flour

2 (10-oz.) cans clams
   (about ¾–1 cup)

1 Tbsp. vinegar

½ cup butter

Bring 3 cups of the milk, clam juice, and salt to a boil in a saucepan over medium-high heat. In the meantime, finely chop vegetables and then add to boiling liquid. Cook for 15–20 minutes until vegetables are tender. In a bowl, mix together flour with the remaining cup of milk and stir into boiling soup. Cook until thick and bubbly. Slice butter into hot chowder and stir until melted. Remove from heat and stir in clams and vinegar. Serve with cornbread.

Jillayne Clements

Vegetable Soup with Dumplings

Makes: about 6 servings   •   Prep: 25 minutes

Cook: 20-25 minutes at medium heat

Ingredients:

3 cups chicken or turkey stock

¼ tsp. garlic powder

½ tsp. onion powder

½ tsp. basil

salt to taste

½ onion, chopped

½ cup carrots, chopped

½ cup shredded cabbage

1 small zucchini, chopped

½ cup green beans, ends cut
   and cut in half

Bring stock to boil with seasonings and then stir in chopped vegetables. Return to a boil and then add dumplings. Cook for 20–25 or until vegetables are nice and tender.

(Pictured with Dumplings on page 58.)

Bloopers

Blooper #1	Cookies

This is what happens when you make cookies only out of improperly prepared rice flour.

Blooper #2	Cream Puffs

This is what happens when cream puffs cool too fast.

Jillayne Clements

Blooper #3 | Corn Tortillas

Attempt #1

Attempt #2

Attempts #3 and #4 not pictured due to tears.

This is what happens when you attempt to make anything with corn without first treating it with lime.

Blooper #4 | Muffins

These muffins are actually cooked. This is what happens when you have too much glue flour and not enough moisture in your recipe.

Blooper #5	Angel Food Cake

This is what happens when you don't fold in the flour to the fluffy egg whites and instead just beat them on high speed and watch in horror as the fluff turns to runniness.

Blooper #6	Injera

This is what happens when you become too confident in your multi-tasking skills and forget you've got something on the stove.

Jillayne Clements

Blooper #7 — Artsian Bread

This is what happens when you don't add enough flour to your artisan bread (or any bread recipe.) It might make a great Frisbee, though.

Blooper #8 — Messy Kitchen

Before   After

This is what happens when you're cooking four recipes a day for several weeks in a row.

RESOURCES

Ideas of where to buy bulk:

The Teff Co.—Great place to buy teff. They have both brown and ivory varieties of teff, and it comes in either whole grain or flour. You may also buy 5 pounds or 25 pounds. (The 25-pound bag is a better deal.) They deliver right to your front door, and the shipping is included in the price.

Website: www.teffco.com.

Lundberg Rice—Grown in California. You may buy bulk directly from their warehouse through a mail-in order. Bulk options are mail-in; smaller packages may be ordered online. Even with shipping, the price per pound is a good deal.

Website: www.lundberg.com.

GF Harvest—Sells certified gluten-free oats in groat form, rolled, or steel-cut. You can buy bulk or smaller packages shipped to your home.

Website: www.glutenfreeoats.com.

Honeyville Grain—Has a variety of different bulk foods such as corn and great northern beans (I use these for sprouted white beans). They also have flax, though it looks like they only offer the darker flax, and I prefer golden because it's more aesthetically pleasing when making bread. If you aren't bothered with the darker kind, this place may be the way to go. They have a $4.49 flat shipping rate.

Website: www.honeyvillegrain.com.

Flax Premium Gold—for golden flaxseed in bulk. Free shipping.

Website: www.flaxpremiumgold.com

Jillayne Clements

Gluten-Free Baking Ingredients

McCormick vanilla—GF

Rumford Baking Soda—GF and aluminum free

Bragg's Liquid Aminos—GF version of soy sauce

Enjoy Life—GF, dairy-free, egg-free, soy-free chocolate chips. They also have other products as well.
  Website: www.enjoylifefoods.com.

Follow Your Heart Vegenaise—GF, egg free, mayonnaise made with healthier ingredients.
  Website: www.followyourheart.com.

Equipment

- Heavy-duty food processor like Hamilton

- Stand mixer

- Stainless steel bowls for soaking and souring

- Glass bowls for soaking and souring

- Food dehydrator with mesh and plastic liners

- Stainless steel colander

- Stainless steel pans (aluminum will corrode into corn when treating it with lime)

- Small food processor or coffee grinder for grinding flax, corn, or any other grain into coarse flours. Great for making cereals, like Cream of Rice. (If you don't drink coffee and are concerned that your ecclesiastical leader might see you at Walmart with one tucked under your arm, you can purchase one online for around $10.00 + S&H.)

- NutriBullet—powerful machine, much like a blender. Great for turning cooked and dehydrated rice to flour in one step, perfect for milling GF flours. Also is powerful enough to make your own nut butters. Also makes smoothies out of whole fruits and vegetables so you can drink the fiber. I use mine multiple times a day.

REFERENCES

1. Sally Fallon and Mary G. Enig, PhD, "Be Kind to Your Grains . . . And Your Grains Will Be Kind To You," January 1, 2000. http://www.westonaprice.org/food-features/be-kind-to-your-grains. Accessed March 25, 2013.

2. Sally Fallon and Mary G. Enig, PhD, "Be Kind to Your Grains . . . And Your Grains Will Be Kind To You." January 1, 2000. http://www.westonaprice.org/food-features/be-kind-to-your-grains. Accessed March 25, 2013.

3. Essentialeating.com, "Digestible Grains and Diabetes." http://essentialeating.com/blogs/sprouted-flour/5713692-digestible-grains-and-diabetes. Accessed March 25, 2013.

4. Kaayla Daniel PhD, CCN, "Plants Bite Back." March 29, 2010. http://www.westonaprice.org/search/search?q=plants+bite+back. Accessed March 25, 2013.

Sally Fallon and Mary G. Enig, PhD, "Be Kind to Your Grains . . . And Your Grains Will Be Kind To You." January 1, 2000. http://www.westonaprice.org/food-features/be-kind-to-your-grains. Accessed March 25, 2013.

5. Fitday.com, "High-fructose Corn Syrup vs. Corn Syrup: The Facts." http://www.fitday.com/fitness-articles/nutrition/healthy-eating/high-fructose-corn-syrup-vs-corn-syrup-the-facts.html#b. Copyright 2000–2011 by Internet Brands. Accessed March 20, 2013.

6. Mary Shomon, "Soy and the Thyroid: A Look at the Controversy over Soy and Thyroid Health." June 12, 2012. http://thyroid.about.com/cs/soyinfo/a/soy_2.htm. Accessed March 29, 2013.

7. Alan Wagner, "Homemade Corn Tortillas." 2002. http://www.greensense.com/Features/Green_cuisine/tortillas.htm. Accessed March 21, 2013.

8. Jillayne Clements and Michelle Stewart. "Traditional Almonds." *The Diet Rebel's Cookbook.* (Springville: Cedar Fort, 2008.) 45. Based on a recipe in: Fallon and Enig, *Nourishing Traditions: The Cookbook that Challenges Politically Correct Nutrition and the Diet Dictocrats*, 515.

Index

About the Author

Jillayne Clements holds a bachelor's degree in family and human development from Utah State University and is an author of both fiction and nonfiction books, including *Deadly Treasure: A Novel*, *The Diet Rebel's Cookbook: Eating Clean and Green*, coauthored with Michelle Stewart, as well as an upcoming novel.

After being diagnosed with Hashimoto's thyroiditis, she studied the importance of whole foods cooking and began creating her own recipes. She has taught classes in her community and at the Young Living Farm, including their yearly Lavender Days events, and has catered for some of their essential oil conventions. She has also made whole foods desserts on both *Good Things Utah* and on *Studio 5*.

Jillayne resides with her husband and children in the shadows of Mt. Nebo, where she enjoys writing fiction, four-wheeling up mountain trails, and growing a lot of her own produce.

For more information, visit her website and blog:

www.jillayneclements.com • www.jillayneclements.blogspot.com